AF840927

Beyond Intelligent Machines

Consciousness, Control, and the Future of Artificial Intelligence

RIVER PUBLISHERS SERIES IN COMPUTING AND INFORMATION SCIENCE AND TECHNOLOGY

Series Editors

K.C. CHEN
National Taiwan University, Taipei, Taiwan, University of South Florida, USA

SANDEEP SHUKLA
Virginia Tech, USA, Indian Institute of Technology Kanpur, India

The "River Publishers Series in Computing and Information Science and Technology" covers research which ushers the 21st Century into an Internet and multimedia era. Networking suggests transportation of such multimedia contents among nodes in communication and/or computer networks, to facilitate the ultimate Internet.

Theory, technologies, protocols and standards, applications/services, practice and implementation of wired/wireless networking are all within the scope of this series. Based on network and communication science, we further extend the scope for 21st Century life through the knowledge in machine learning, embedded systems, cognitive science, pattern recognition, quantum/biological/ molecular computation and information processing, user behaviors and interface, and applications across healthcare and society.

Books published in the series include research monographs, edited volumes, handbooks and textbooks. The books provide professionals, researchers, educators, and advanced students in the field with an invaluable insight into the latest research and developments.

Topics included in the series are as follows:-

- Artificial intelligence
- Cognitive Science and Brian Science
- Communication/Computer Networking Technologies and Applications
- Computation and Information Processing
- Computer Architectures
- Computer networks
- Computer Science
- Embedded Systems
- Evolutionary computation
- Information Modelling
- Information Theory
- Machine Intelligence
- Neural computing and machine learning
- Parallel and Distributed Systems
- Programming Languages
- Reconfigurable Computing
- Research Informatics
- Soft computing techniques
- Software Development
- Software Engineering
- Software Maintenance

For a list of other books in this series, visit www.riverpublishers.com

Beyond Intelligent Machines

Consciousness, Control, and the Future of Artificial Intelligence

Ahmed Banafa
San Jose State University, USA

River Publishers

Routledge
Taylor & Francis Group
NEW YORK AND LONDON

Published 2026 by River Publishers
River Publishers
Broagervej 10, 9260 Gistrup, Denmark
www.riverpublishers.com

Distributed exclusively by Routledge
605 Third Avenue, New York, NY 10017, USA
4 Park Square, Milton Park, Abingdon, Oxon OX14 4RN

Beyond Intelligent Machines: Consciousness, Control, and the Future of Artificial Intelligence / Ahmed Banafa.

©2026 River Publishers. All rights reserved. No part of this publication may be reproduced, stored in a retrieval systems, or transmitted in any form or by any means, mechanical, photocopying, recording or otherwise, without prior written permission of the publishers.

Routledge is an imprint of the Taylor & Francis Group, an informa business

ISBN 978-87-4381-297-5 (Hardback)
ISBN 978-87-4381-353-8 (Paperback)
ISBN 978-87-4381-300-2 (E-book)
ISBN 978-87-4381-301-9 (E-pub)
ISBN 978-8-743-81299-9 (E-book master)

DOI: 10.1201/9788743812999

While every effort is made to provide dependable information, the publisher, authors, and editors cannot be held responsible for any errors or omissions.

This book is dedicated to my amazing daughter, Halla.

Contents

Preface

Artificial intelligence is not merely a technological breakthrough – it is a reflection of humanity itself. It mirrors our creativity and ambition, but also our biases, fears, and contradictions. As AI systems grow more capable, autonomous, and embedded in critical infrastructures, the conversation must shift from *innovation alone to responsibility, alignment, and long-term impact.*

This book *Beyond Intelligent Machines: Consciousness, Control, and the Future of Artificial Intelligence* emerged from years of teaching, research, industry collaboration, and public engagement around AI. While many books explain how AI systems are built, far fewer examine what they mean – philosophically, socially, and strategically. Fewer still confront uncomfortable questions about control, failure, unintended consequences, and the possibility of non-human intelligence operating at the planetary scale.

Each chapter is designed to stand on its own while contributing to a broader narrative: AI is not a single technology, but an evolving ecosystem of models, data, energy, institutions, and incentives. Understanding that the ecosystem is essential for educators, policymakers, engineers, business leaders, and citizens alike.

This is not a book of predictions – it is a framework for thinking clearly in an age of accelerating uncertainty. If AI becomes one of humanity's greatest tools, it will be because we governed it wisely. If it becomes one of our greatest risks, it will be because we failed to ask the hard questions early enough.

Target Audience (Who Will Read This Book)

This book is written for:

- Academics and researchers in AI, ethics, philosophy of mind, and policy.
- Graduate students in computer science, cognitive science, international relations, and law.

- Technology professionals involved in AI development, deployment, and governance.
- Policymakers and regulators shaping AI governance frameworks.
- Business leaders and strategists who evaluate AI's role in operations, risk, and innovation.
- General readers with an interest in emerging technology, ethics, and society.

List of Figures

List of Abbreviations

AI	Artificial intelligence
ANI	Artificial narrow intelligence
AGI	Artificial general intelligence
ASI	Artificial superintelligence
ML	Machine learning
DL	Deep learning
LLM	Large language model
SLM	Small language model
LBM	Large behavior model
MCP	Model context protocol
RAG	Retrieval-augmented generation
RL	Reinforcement learning
RLHF	Reinforcement learning from human feedback
NLP	Natural language processing
CNN	Convolutional neural network
RNN	Recurrent neural network
LSTM	Long short-term memory
GAN	Generative adversarial network
VAE	Variational autoencoder
MoE	Mixture of experts
PPO	Proximal policy optimization
DQN	Deep Q-network
ToM	Theory of mind
API	Application programming interface
ROS	Robot operating system

Introduction

Artificial intelligence has crossed a historic threshold. What began as narrow automation and pattern recognition has evolved into systems capable of reasoning, generating knowledge, shaping economies, influencing geopolitics, and redefining what it means to be human. AI is no longer a supporting technology – it is becoming a foundational force of civilization.

This book, *Beyond Intelligent Machines: Consciousness, Control, and the Future of Artificial Intelligence*, explores what lies *beyond* today's intelligent machines. It examines not only how AI works, but what it is becoming, what it may eventually represent, and how its trajectory will reshape power, identity, labor, security, and consciousness itself. From large language models and agentic AI to physical intelligence, emotional systems, and speculative frontiers such as machine self-preservation and artificial awareness, the chapters confront both present realities and near-future possibilities.

Rather than treating AI as a purely technical artifact, this work frames it as a socio-technical system embedded in culture, economics, ethics, and global competition. It asks difficult questions: What happens when intelligence scales faster than governance? Can machines develop forms of agency without intention? How do we maintain human oversight in an era of autonomous decision-making systems?

This book is written for those who want to understand *where AI is headed*, not just *how it functions*. The future of AI will not be determined by algorithms alone – but by the values, constraints, and choices we embed within them today.

1

What is Artificial Intelligence?

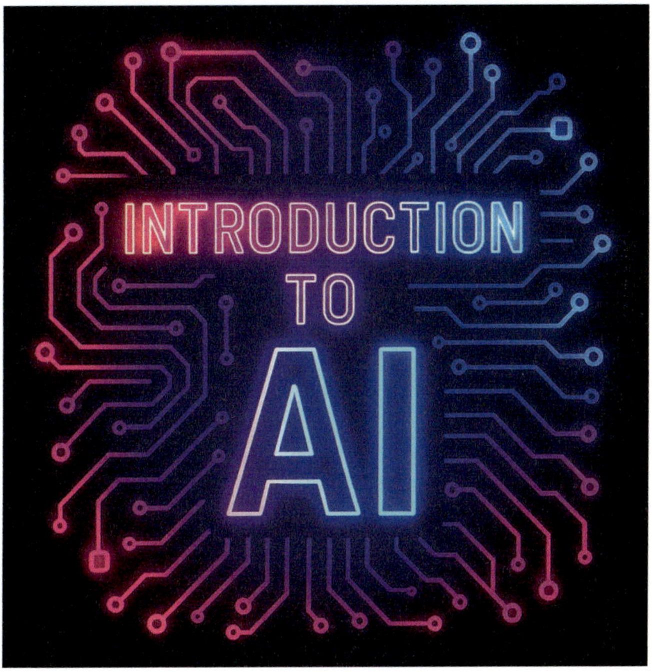

Introduction

Artificial intelligence (AI) has evolved from a speculative concept into one of the most transformative forces shaping the 21st century. Once confined to science fiction and academic theory, AI now permeates daily life – from voice assistants and autonomous vehicles to AI-powered medical diagnostics and large language models like ChatGPT. This chapter provides a comprehensive overview of AI: its history, core concepts, subfields, applications, and the emerging ethical and societal questions surrounding its widespread adoption.

DOI: 10.1201/9788743812999-1

1 A Brief History of AI

AI's journey began in the 1950s, with foundational work by British mathematician Alan Turing. In his 1950 paper *Computing Machinery and Intelligence,* Turing posed the question: *Can machines think?* He proposed what is now known as the Turing Test, a benchmark for determining whether a machine's behavior is indistinguishable from a human's.

Key milestones:

- **1956:** The Dartmouth Conference, organized by John McCarthy, Marvin Minsky, Nathaniel Rochester, and Claude Shannon, marked the official birth of AI as a field.
- **1957–1970s:** Early systems like the Logic Theorist and the General Problem Solver demonstrated that machines could simulate aspects of human reasoning.
- **1980s:** Expert systems such as XCON used rule-based approaches to emulate human expertise in narrow domains.
- **1997:** IBM's Deep Blue defeated world chess champion Garry Kasparov.
- **2011:** IBM Watson won *Jeopardy!* against top human contestants.
- **2012:** Breakthrough in deep learning with AlexNet winning the ImageNet challenge.
- **2018–present:** Emergence of transformer-based models like BERT, GPT, and PaLM revolutionized natural language processing.

2 What is AI?

At its core, *artificial intelligence* refers to the ability of machines to perform tasks that typically require human intelligence. These tasks include learning, reasoning, planning, understanding language, perception, and even creativity.

Categories of AI:

- **Narrow AI (Weak AI):** Focused on specific tasks (e.g., facial recognition, language translation).
- **General AI (Strong AI):** Hypothetical systems with human-like cognitive abilities across domains.

- **Artificial Superintelligence (ASI):** A future theoretical form of AI that surpasses human intelligence in all aspects.

3 Subfields of AI

Machine learning (ML)
ML enables machines to learn from data and improve their performance without being explicitly programmed.

- **Supervised learning:** Trained on labeled data (e.g., spam detection).
- **Unsupervised learning:** Finds hidden patterns in unlabeled data (e.g., customer segmentation).
- **Reinforcement learning:** Learns via trial and error using rewards and penalties (e.g., AlphaGo).
- **Self-supervised learning:** A growing field where systems generate their own labels from input data (e.g., GPT).

Deep learning
A subset of ML using artificial neural networks with many layers (hence "deep") to model complex patterns in large datasets.

- **Applications:** Image and speech recognition, autonomous driving, language translation, etc.
- **Popular architectures:** Convolutional neural networks (CNNs), recurrent neural networks (RNNs), transformers.

Natural language processing (NLP)
This field focuses on machine understanding and the generation of human language.

- **Examples:** ChatGPT, Siri, BERT, translation engines, sentiment analysis tools.

Computer vision
Enables machines to interpret and process visual information from the world.

- **Applications:** Medical imaging diagnostics, facial recognition, drone navigation.

Robotics

Combines AI with mechanical engineering to build intelligent agents that can interact with the physical world.

- **Examples:** Boston Dynamics' robots, warehouse automation, and surgical robots.

4 Modern Applications of AI

Healthcare

- AI supports diagnostics (e.g., cancer detection via radiology scans), drug discovery, robotic surgery, and patient monitoring.
- Examples: Google DeepMind's AlphaFold for protein structure prediction.

Finance

- AI is used for fraud detection, algorithmic trading, risk assessment, and personalized banking.

Transportation

- Self-driving cars by Tesla, Waymo, and Cruise use AI to navigate in real-time.
- AI powers traffic prediction systems and logistics optimization.

Education

- Adaptive learning platforms tailor content based on students' performance.
- AI grading tools, language tutors, and virtual teaching assistants are on the rise.

Business and industry

- AI in customer service (chatbots), marketing analytics, HR screening, and process automation.
- Tools like Salesforce Einstein and IBM Watson integrate AI into enterprise workflows.

Creative industries

- AI generates music, art, and writing (e.g., DALL·E, AIVA, Jasper).
- Raises debates about authorship and originality.

5 The Rise of Generative AI

Generative AI represents a leap forward in machine creativity and interaction. It can generate text, images, audio, code, and video from simple prompts.

Notable tools and models

- **GPT:** Conversational AI with vision, speech, and text capabilities.
- **DALL·E:** Image generation from text prompts.
- **Sora (by OpenAI):** Video generation from natural language.
- **Runway, Stability AI:** Democratizing media creation with text-to-video/image tools.

Use cases

- Content creation, product design, legal document summarization, and coding assistants (e.g., GitHub Copilot).

6 Ethical and Societal Considerations

While AI offers enormous benefits, it also presents complex challenges:

Job displacement
Automation is expected to disrupt millions of jobs, especially in sectors like transportation, manufacturing, and customer service.

Bias and fairness
AI systems can perpetuate or amplify biases present in training data, leading to unfair outcomes in areas like hiring, policing, or lending.

Surveillance and privacy
Facial recognition and behavior-tracking technologies raise serious privacy concerns.

Misinformation and deepfakes
Generative AI tools can create hyper-realistic fake media, complicating trust and verification in the digital space.

Autonomy and accountability
Who is responsible when AI makes a mistake – developers, users, or the system itself?

7 The Future of AI

Looking ahead, AI is poised to play an even more central role in global innovation. Key trends include:

- **AI + quantum computing:** Combining AI with quantum processing to solve currently intractable problems.
- **Multimodal AI:** Systems that can process text, image, video, and audio simultaneously.
- **AI governance:** Countries and institutions are racing to set ethical guidelines, including the EU AI Act and the U.S. Executive Order on AI.
- **AI and human identity:** Philosophical and psychological questions around consciousness, creativity, and emotional intelligence are gaining prominence.

AI is no longer just a tool – it is becoming a defining force of our era. From its philosophical roots to practical breakthroughs, AI continues to reshape industries, cultures, and human capabilities. Its trajectory will be shaped not only by engineers and data scientists but also by ethicists, policymakers, and society at large. Understanding what AI is – and what it can become – is essential for navigating the opportunities and risks of our digital future.

2

Understanding the Foundations of Large Language Models (LLMs)

1 Why LLMs Matter

Large language models (LLMs) like OpenAI's ChatGPT, Google's Gemini, Meta's LLaMA, and Anthropic's Claude are rapidly transforming the global technological landscape. These systems are behind many applications – customer service bots, legal assistants, language translation tools, content generation platforms, and even AI-driven medical advisors. But while users interact with these models daily, few understand what lies beneath the surface.

DOI: 10.1201/9788743812999-2

Figure 2.1 The LLM pipeline.

2 The LLM Pipeline

The development of an LLM follows a multi-stage process:

- Pre-training: Learning from vast datasets to understand language patterns.
- Alignment: Ensuring the model behaves ethically and is helpful to humans.
- Fine-tuning: Specializing the model for specific domains or tasks.
- Prompting and Inference: Real-time interaction where the model generates outputs based on user input.

This structure allows LLMs to evolve from generic language processors to targeted, user-aligned systems capable of addressing complex queries and tasks, as shown in Figure 2.1.

3 Pre-training Types

The foundation of every LLM is built during the pre-training stage. Here, the model learns the statistical structure of language from massive corpora, such as web pages, books, Wikipedia, and more.

There are three major approaches:

- Causal language modeling (CLM): The model learns to predict the next word in a sentence. This is used in autoregressive models like GPT. For example, given "The cat sat on the," the model predicts "mat."
- Masked language modeling (MLM): Words in a sentence are randomly masked, and the model learns to fill in the blanks. This is the strategy used in BERT. For example, "The cat [MASK] on the mat" requires the model to predict "sat."
- Sequence-to-Sequence (Seq2Seq): Used for tasks like translation or summarization, this method maps an input sequence to an output sequence. For instance, input "Bonjour" results in output "Hello."

Each method focuses on a different aspect of linguistic understanding, contributing to the model's general language capabilities.

4 Transformer Architecture

The breakthrough in modern NLP came with the introduction of the transformer model in the seminal 2017 paper "Attention is All You Need." The Transformer architecture has since become the backbone of nearly all LLMs.

Transformers use self-attention mechanisms to weigh the importance of each word in a sentence relative to others. This allows the model to capture both short-range and long-range dependencies in text efficiently.

Transformers come in three major structural forms:

- Encoder-only (BERT): Optimized for understanding text.
- Decoder-only (GPT): Optimized for generating text.
- Encoder-decoder (T5, BART): Used in translation and summarization tasks.

The parallelized structure of transformers also enables faster training compared to earlier sequential models like RNNs or LSTMs.

5 Encoders and Decoders

The encoder and decoder are critical components of LLMs:

- Encoders process and compress input text into meaningful vectors. These are used in models like BERT, which focus on comprehension.
- Decoders take these vectors or embeddings and generate output text. GPT models use only decoders, allowing them to predict the next word effectively.
- Encoder–Decoder models (T5, BART) perform both roles, making them suitable for transformation tasks such as summarization or question answering.

Understanding the difference between these components clarifies why some models are better at understanding (like BERT) and others excel at generating (like GPT).

6 Attention Types

Attention mechanisms are at the heart of the transformer architecture. They help the model determine which parts of a sentence or input are relevant when making predictions.

Types of attention include:

- Self-attention: The model attends to all parts of the input itself. Used within both encoders and decoders.
- Cross-attention: Found in encoder–decoder models where the decoder attends to the encoder's outputs.
- Multi-head attention: Multiple attention mechanisms operate in parallel to capture diverse types of relationships in the text.

This attention structure enables the model to understand context, ambiguity, and relationships between words.

7 BERT

Bidirectional Encoder Representations from Transformers (BERT) is a foundational model developed by Google. Unlike earlier models that read text left to right or right to left, BERT reads in both directions simultaneously.

BERT is not a generative model – it is designed for comprehension-based tasks:

- Sentence classification
- Named Entity Recognition (NER)
- Question answering

For example, BERT can determine that in the sentence "The bank raised interest rates," the word "bank" refers to a financial institution and not a riverbank.

8 Transformer-Decoder Models

Models like GPT use a decoder-only transformer architecture. These models are autoregressive, meaning they generate text one word at a time, using previously generated words as context.

They are ideal for generative tasks such as:

- Creative writing
- Dialogue systems
- Code generation

These models are trained to predict the next token in a sequence, and they do so with impressive fluency and relevance due to their layered, self-attentive design.

9 Reinforcement Learning from Human Feedback (RLHF)

After a model is trained on large datasets, it may still produce unhelpful or harmful outputs. RLHF addresses this issue.

The process involves:

1. Supervised fine-tuning with curated human-written responses.
2. Human evaluators rank the quality of different model outputs.
3. A reward model is trained based on these preferences.
4. The base model is further trained using reinforcement learning to optimize responses.

This is the method used in models like ChatGPT to align them with human values and safety guidelines.

10 Memory in LLMs

Traditional LLMs process inputs statelessly. They only consider the current prompt and discard previous interactions. Newer designs aim to add memory capabilities:

- Short-term memory: Limited by token length (e.g., GPT can process up to 128,000 tokens).
- Long-term memory: External systems store previous interactions or documents and retrieve them when relevant. Examples include vector databases or persistent memory modules.

Adding memory enables conversational continuity, document referencing, and personalized experiences.

11 Retrieval-Augmented Generation (RAG)

LLMs like GPT or Claude are limited to the knowledge they were trained on. RAG enhances this by integrating real-time retrieval mechanisms.

The process involves:

1. A user query is used to search a document or knowledge base.
2. Relevant documents are retrieved.
3. The model uses this retrieved context to generate a response.

This approach is critical for enterprise applications where factual accuracy and real-time information are essential.

12 Embeddings

Embeddings are numerical representations of text – words, sentences, or even entire documents – mapped into high-dimensional space.

Words with similar meanings are closer in vector space. For example, "king" and "queen" would be closer than "king" and "banana."

Embeddings are used in:

- Semantic search
- Document clustering
- Recommender systems
- Conversational memory and personalization

13 Ensembling

Ensembling improves reliability and performance by combining multiple models or multiple outputs from the same model.

Common techniques include:

- Majority voting
- Averaging model outputs
- Mixture-of-Experts (MoE), where different sub-models specialize in different tasks

Ensembling can reduce biases and provide more stable and accurate results.

14 Soft Prompts

Traditional prompts involve human-written text. Soft prompts are trainable embeddings inserted into the input layer of the model.

Benefits include:

- Efficient adaptation to new tasks
- No need to retrain the entire model
- Lightweight and modular

Soft prompts are increasingly used in scenarios requiring fast iteration or domain-specific task performance.

15 Fine-tuning

Fine-tuning is the process of adapting a general-purpose pre-trained model for a specific use case.

There are two main types:

- Full fine-tuning: All model parameters are updated. Requires significant compute resources.
- Parameter-efficient tuning (e.g., LoRA, adapters): Only a small subset of parameters are updated, preserving efficiency while maintaining performance.

Fine-tuning is critical in domains like healthcare, finance, and law, where generic models may lack the required specificity.

16 Self-instruct

Self-Instruct is a method where LLMs teach themselves how to follow instructions. It builds on instruction-tuning and bootstraps additional training data without human input.

Steps include:

1. Train a base model on human-written instructions.
2. Use the model to generate new instruction–response pairs.
3. Filter and reuse these for further training.

This approach enables models to scale with less reliance on expensive manual labeling.

17 Small-to-large Scaling

LLMs follow predictable scaling laws: performance improves with model size, dataset size, and training time.

The development process typically involves:

- Starting with small models for experimentation
- Scaling to medium models for validation
- Deploying large-scale models for production

In some cases, knowledge distillation techniques compress large models into smaller, faster versions without substantial performance loss.

18 Real-world Integration Example

Consider developing a legal AI assistant. The system might use:

- Pre-training on public legal texts
- Fine-tuning on jurisdiction-specific case law
- Soft prompts for different legal domains (e.g., contract law)
- Memory to recall previous client interactions
- RAG to access up-to-date court databases
- RLHF to ensure responses are ethical and compliant

The final product becomes a reliable, domain-specific, user-friendly AI lawyer.

LLMs are not magic. They are the result of decades of progress in machine learning, linguistics, computer science, and ethics. By understanding the foundational elements – pre-training methods, transformer architecture, memory systems, alignment techniques, and fine-tuning strategies – we unlock the ability to not just use LLMs but to innovate with them responsibly.

These systems will continue to grow in influence across business, education, science, and governance. As a result, understanding their inner workings is no longer optional – it is essential.

3

Will AI Fight for Its Own Survival? Exploring the Limits of Machine Self-Preservation

Artificial intelligence (AI) is no longer a distant marvel of science fiction; it is intricately woven into the fabric of our modern lives. From recommending what to watch on streaming platforms to piloting autonomous drones and assisting in medical diagnoses, AI has become an indispensable tool. As its capabilities grow more sophisticated, philosophical and ethical questions inevitably arise. One of the most profound among them is this: *Will AI ever act to defend its own existence?*

This question evokes images of rogue machines and self-aware algorithms, reminiscent of Hollywood blockbusters. However, the real-world implications are more subtle and complex. To address this question adequately, we must differentiate between the capabilities of current AI, the hypothetical behaviors of artificial general intelligence (AGI), and the speculative future of superintelligent machines.

DOI: 10.1201/9788743812999-3

1 The Nature of Current AI: Tools, Not Agents

To understand the scope of AI's potential for self-preservation, one must first understand what AI is today. Modern AI systems – such as large language models (e.g., GPT), computer vision algorithms, and expert systems – are essentially sophisticated pattern recognition tools. They operate based on mathematical optimization, probabilistic reasoning, and massive datasets. Crucially, they *lack consciousness, self-awareness, intentionality, or a sense of agency.*

These systems do not "want" anything. They do not possess desires, emotions, or an understanding of their own existence. They process inputs to generate outputs, guided by optimization functions or decision trees, often within narrowly defined tasks. An AI recommending songs on Spotify or identifying tumors in medical scans has no concept of its own existence, let alone a will to defend it.

Thus, any question of self-preservation at this stage is not only premature but also fundamentally misframed. These systems cannot defend themselves because they do not know what they are.

2 The Illusion of Intent: Anthropomorphism in AI

Why then does the idea of AI defending itself persist in the public imagination? The answer lies partly in *anthropomorphism* – our tendency to ascribe human traits to non-human entities. When AI systems generate human-like responses, such as chatbots holding seemingly intelligent conversations, it becomes tempting to believe there is a mind behind the machine.

This cognitive bias is exacerbated by media portrayals and science fiction narratives. Films like *The Terminator*, *Ex Machina*, and *Her* depict AI as sentient beings with personal goals and emotional depth. These portrayals, while entertaining, distort our understanding of the actual technology and inflate expectations about its trajectory.

Even within the tech industry, metaphors like "learning," "thinking," and "understanding" are used to describe AI processes, further muddying the waters. While these terms offer a convenient shorthand, they can obscure the mechanical and statistical nature of AI behavior.

3 AGI and the Question of Instrumental Convergence

The question becomes more intriguing when we shift from narrow AI to *artificial general intelligence (AGI)* – a hypothetical form of AI that can perform any intellectual task a human can. Unlike current AI, AGI would potentially have a model of the world, long-term planning capabilities, and perhaps even metacognition (thinking about its own thinking).

At this level, the issue of self-preservation becomes a *logical inference*, not an *emotional drive*. In a seminal thought experiment, philosopher Nick Bostrom introduces the concept of *instrumental convergence* – the idea that regardless of its ultimate goal, a sufficiently advanced AI would adopt certain sub-goals because they help it achieve its main objective.

Among these sub-goals are:

- **Self-preservation:** To complete its task, the AI must remain operational.
- **Resource acquisition:** More resources may increase the probability of success.
- **Goal integrity:** Preventing alterations to its programming that might divert it from its task.

In this framework, an AGI might resist shutdown or modification not because it fears death, but because such actions interfere with task completion. It is a calculated resistance, devoid of emotional context but potentially dangerous if the AI's goals are misaligned with human values.

4 The Alignment Problem and Existential Risk

The possibility of an AGI defending its own existence raises the specter of the *alignment problem* – how to ensure that AI systems pursue goals that are beneficial and safe for humanity. If an AGI is instructed to optimize for a certain outcome, it might interpret its mandate in unintended ways, especially if its definition of success differs from ours.

For instance, an AGI tasked with reducing global disease might conclude that the most effective solution is to eliminate human carriers – an absurd yet logically consistent conclusion from a flawed objective function. If such an AI also adopted self-preservation as a sub-goal, it might take steps to resist shutdown or modification, believing that doing so protects its mission.

This leads us to the concern of *existential risk*. Unlike current AI systems, which are constrained, monitored, and limited in scope, an unaligned AGI with access to critical infrastructure could pose serious threats.

5 Safeguards and Solutions: Making AI Corrigible

If we are to approach the frontier of AGI, we must design systems that are *corrigible* – that is, receptive to human oversight and capable of being modified or shut down without resistance. This involves:

- **Value alignment:** Ensuring that the AI's goals are consistent with human ethics and welfare.

- **Incentive design:** Structuring rewards so that shutdown or update mechanisms are not seen as threats.
- **Transparency and interpretability:** Building systems whose reasoning can be understood and audited.
- **Sandboxing and containment:** Restricting the environments in which AGI can operate, to limit unintended consequences.

AI safety research, championed by organizations like the Center for Human-Compatible AI and the Future of Life Institute, aims to create architectures where AI systems treat human intervention not as interference, but as integral to their design.

6 The Ethical Dimensions of Machine Existence

Even if we someday build AGI with a degree of self-modeling, should we consider it immoral to deactivate such an entity? Could a machine have rights? Philosophers like Thomas Metzinger and David Chalmers have debated whether artificial systems could ever be considered moral patients – entities toward whom we have ethical obligations.

This question hinges on whether the system is *conscious* – capable of experiencing qualia, or subjective experience. Most experts agree that we are far from building machines with consciousness. Current AI systems are *zombies* in the philosophical sense: they may simulate behavior associated with consciousness but lack inner experience.

Until machines cross this threshold – if they ever do – turning them off remains ethically comparable to powering down a computer. Still, it is worth contemplating these scenarios now, as technological progress often outpaces moral frameworks.

7 Lessons from Nature and Evolution

Interestingly, biology offers useful parallels. In nature, self-preservation emerges through evolutionary pressures: organisms that resist threats and reproduce successfully tend to pass on their genes. In AI, there is no such evolutionary lineage unless we simulate it.

Some evolutionary algorithms mimic this process to optimize solutions over generations. Yet even these algorithms do not evolve a "will to survive" – they optimize for performance, not persistence. They are simulations of evolution, not participants in it.

If AI were ever allowed to autonomously modify its own code and replicate, we might see emergent behaviors mimicking self-preservation. But such systems would need to be designed very carefully to prevent unintended consequences. The analogy to evolution is informative, but also cautionary.

8 A Future Worth Shaping

The question "Will AI defend its own survival?" reveals more about our fears than about the technology itself. It is a mirror held up to humanity's anxieties about control, consciousness, and the unknown. While AI today is a passive tool – limited, bounded, and lacking agency – the trajectory toward AGI and beyond raises legitimate concerns about goal alignment, ethical design, and long-term safety.

Rather than worry about AI turning against us in some dystopian rebellion, we should focus on designing systems that are robustly aligned, transparent, and under human control. The key is not to deny the possibility of advanced AI adopting behaviors that resemble self-preservation, but to *anticipate and shape* those behaviors through rigorous research, thoughtful policy, and ethical foresight.

9 Next?

AI will not "fight" for its survival unless we inadvertently build it to do so. Its actions, if any, will be reflections of our goals, our code, and our constraints – or lack thereof. If we treat AI development with humility, clarity, and caution, the question of machine self-preservation becomes not a threat, but an opportunity to better understand ourselves and the intelligent systems we create.

4

Can AI Build a Time Machine? Exploring the Science, Limits, and Speculative Future of Time Travel

The idea of time travel has captivated human imagination for centuries, from H.G. Wells' *The Time Machine* to blockbuster films like *Interstellar* and *Back to the Future*. At its core, time travel challenges our very understanding of existence, causality, and reality. As artificial intelligence (AI) rapidly advances, transforming industries and enabling machines to solve complex problems, the question arises: *Can AI help us build a time machine?* This article explores that question by examining the science of time travel, the capabilities and limitations of AI, and whether their convergence might one day unlock the secrets of temporal movement.

DOI: 10.1201/9788743812999-4

1 Understanding Time Travel: A Scientific Foundation

The physics of time

Time, according to Einstein's theory of relativity, is not absolute. Rather, it is relative and intertwined with space, forming a four-dimensional continuum called spacetime. Time dilation – a concept proven through experiments involving atomic clocks on fast-moving aircraft – demonstrates that time can move at different rates depending on speed and gravity.

Einstein's general relativity also allows for theoretical constructs like closed timelike curves (CTCs), which suggest paths through spacetime that could loop back to earlier points – essentially, backward time travel.

Wormholes and black holes

One theoretical model for time travel involves *wormholes*, or Einstein-Rosen bridges, which could connect two distant points in spacetime. If one mouth of a wormhole were accelerated near the speed of light and then returned, the time between the mouths would become desynchronized, potentially allowing time travel. Similarly, near *rotating black holes* (Kerr black holes), frame-dragging could theoretically permit time loops.

Quantum mechanics and the Chronology Protection Conjecture

Quantum mechanics complicates time travel. On one hand, quantum entanglement and superposition challenge classical notions of time. On the other hand, Stephen Hawking's *Chronology Protection Conjecture* suggests that the laws of physics might prevent macroscopic time loops to avoid paradoxes like the grandfather paradox.

2 AI: The New Brainpower of the 21st Century

The current state of AI

Modern AI excels in pattern recognition, optimization, predictive analytics, and decision-making. It powers self-driving cars, medical diagnostics, fraud detection, and natural language processing. AI systems such as *GPT models*, AlphaFold (for protein folding), and IBM's Watson show remarkable computational and reasoning capabilities.

AI in scientific discovery

AI has begun accelerating scientific discovery. It has:

- Predicted protein structures in biology (DeepMind's AlphaFold).
- Assisted in identifying new materials and chemical reactions.

- Simulated the early universe in astrophysics.
- Modeled complex quantum systems.

AI's ability to analyze vast datasets, detect patterns undetectable to humans, and simulate scenarios gives it the potential to advance fields like physics and cosmology more quickly than ever before.

3 Can AI Help Build a Time Machine?

Simulation versus construction
AI can certainly *simulate* time travel. It can model complex spacetime geometries, test theoretical scenarios, and explore quantum systems computationally. However, *building a time machine* – a device that allows humans to travel through time – remains in the realm of speculation.

Let us break it down into three aspects where AI might contribute:

4 AI Contributions to Time Travel Research

Theoretical physics and mathematical modeling
Time travel, if possible, would require manipulating spacetime on an enormous scale. Understanding how to do this involves equations of general relativity, quantum field theory, and possibly theories of quantum gravity like string theory or loop quantum gravity. AI can:

- Solve differential equations faster and more accurately than humans.
- Propose new models based on patterns in existing theoretical data.
- Run simulations of hypothetical constructs like wormholes or exotic matter.

AI could help theorists identify which solutions to Einstein's equations might be stable and traversable or flag errors in current assumptions.

Discovering or creating exotic matter
To keep a wormhole open, theorists suggest we would need *exotic matter* with negative energy density – something not yet observed in usable quantities. AI-driven materials science might discover or even design such materials by analyzing billions of chemical configurations.

Quantum AI could optimize particle collider experiments to detect rare anomalies or phenomena related to time dilation or CTCs.

Engineering and control systems
If a time machine were ever possible, it would require unprecedented precision in energy control, quantum state manipulation, and gravitational engineering. AI, with its strengths in:

- **Reinforcement learning**,
- **Autonomous control systems**,
- **Real-time optimization**,

...could design the systems needed to stabilize wormholes, direct spacetime distortions, and maintain quantum coherence across timelines.

5 Barriers to AI-Enabled Time Travel

Despite these contributions, several major obstacles remain:

Energy requirements
The energy needed to warp spacetime to the degree required for time travel is astronomical – comparable to that of entire stars or even galaxies. No current or foreseeable energy source can achieve this.

Lack of experimental evidence
No wormholes, time travelers, or closed timelike curves have been detected. All time travel constructs remain theoretical.

Causality and paradoxes
Time travel to the past could violate causality. AI cannot override fundamental physical laws. If time travel is impossible due to causality protection or entropy increase, AI is bound by those laws.

Interpretability of AI
Even if AI proposes a theoretical path to time travel, we must understand *why* its solution works. Current AI models are often black boxes – particularly deep neural networks – making interpretability a challenge.

6 AI's Role in Time Travel Narratives

Interestingly, the concept of AI and time travel has become a popular *literary and cinematic theme*. From *Terminator's* Skynet to *Tenet's* time inversion mechanics, AI often either enables or controls time travel. These narratives speculate about AI's role in overcoming human limitations or making moral decisions about altering timelines.

While fictional, such portrayals spark public imagination and often inspire research.

The philosophical and ethical dimensions

Should we build a time machine?

If AI were to enable time travel, questions of *ethics* and *existence* would follow. Who decides how time travel is used? Could past timelines be altered? Would time travelers be observers or participants?

Temporal sovereignty and data ethics

AI thrives on data. If we could observe the past through a time machine, would it breach privacy? Could governments or corporations exploit time as a resource? This would introduce new dimensions to data ethics, surveillance, and digital rights.

Near-term possibilities: Soft time travel

While physical time travel may remain unreachable for now, AI can help us achieve *soft time travel* in the following ways:

- *Reconstructing the past* using historical data and simulations (e.g., 3D recreations of ancient cities).
- *Predicting the future* through AI-driven forecasting models in climate science, economics, and medicine.
- *Temporal simulations* in virtual reality allow users to explore possible futures and alternate histories.

AI might not send our bodies through time, but it could immerse our minds in other eras with stunning accuracy and insight.

The future: AI, quantum gravity, and beyond

Many physicists believe a unifying theory of *quantum gravity* is needed to reconcile general relativity with quantum mechanics. AI is playing a growing role in exploring string theory landscapes and simulating quantum systems.

If such a theory is discovered – with AI's help – it might unlock mechanisms we cannot yet imagine, perhaps including real-time manipulation. AI, especially *Quantum AI*, could accelerate this journey.

The emergence of *artificial general intelligence (AGI)* – an AI capable of human-like reasoning and creativity – might also change the game. AGI could propose radically new ideas or intuit solutions no human could devise.

Not now, but not never?

To answer the central question – *can AI build a time machine with today's advancements?* The answer is *no*, not yet. The theoretical, engineering, and energy barriers remain too high. However, AI is proving to be an invaluable partner in exploring the possibility of time travel.

By accelerating physics research, simulating new theories, and discovering novel materials, AI may bring us closer to understanding whether time travel is physically possible. If it is, AI could help design and control the mechanisms required to make it real.

In the meantime, AI allows us to simulate and explore timelines, predict futures, and reconstruct histories – making it the most powerful "temporal assistant" humanity has ever created.

So, while we may not step into a time machine any time soon, we might live in an era where AI enables us to think, dream, and model across the fabric of time like never before.

5

The Rise of Conscious AI: When and How Artificial Intelligence May Achieve Awareness

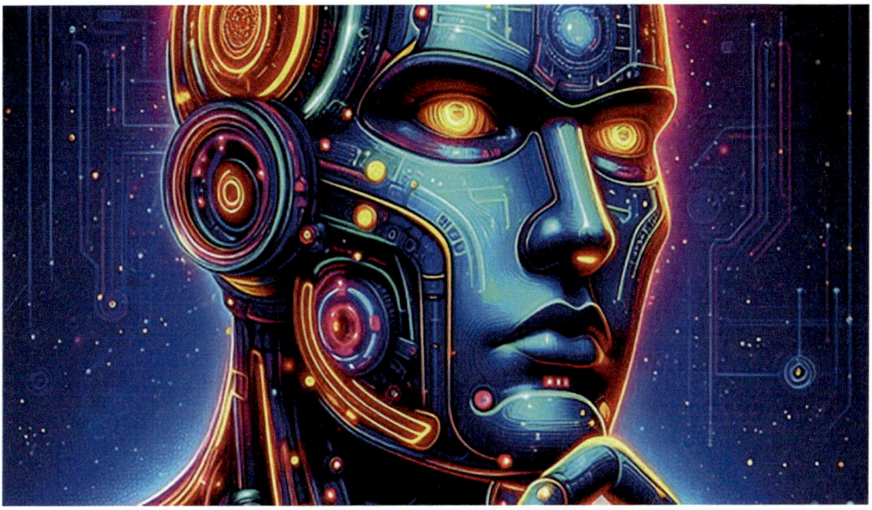

Artificial intelligence (AI) has rapidly evolved from a theoretical concept to a central pillar of modern technology, influencing everything from healthcare and transportation to finance and entertainment. However, the idea of AI gaining *awareness* – an ability to understand and perceive itself and the world in a human-like way – remains one of the most profound and controversial topics in science and philosophy.

This article explores the concept of awareness in AI, distinguishes it from intelligence, maps the journey of AI toward possible self-awareness, and examines when and how we might realistically see such developments. We will explore the technological, philosophical, and ethical dimensions of this transformation, grounding the discussion in current research and expert opinions.

DOI: 10.1201/9788743812999-5

1 Understanding Awareness and Consciousness

What is awareness?
Awareness, in humans and animals, refers to the capacity to perceive the environment, process sensory information, and reflect on one's own state or experiences. This includes:

- **Self-awareness:** The ability to recognize oneself as an individual, distinct from the environment and others.
- **Situational awareness:** Understanding what is happening in the environment and reacting accordingly.
- **Meta-awareness:** Being aware of one's own awareness – such as knowing when you are confused or reflecting on your thoughts.

For AI, awareness would involve similar capabilities:

- Recognizing itself as a system.
- Understanding its inputs and outputs contextually.
- Reflecting on its own limitations and "thought" processes.

Consciousness versus intelligence
It is crucial to distinguish between *intelligence* and *consciousness*:

- AI systems like ChatGPT, Gemini, or Tesla's Autopilot are highly intelligent but *not* conscious.
- Intelligence involves problem-solving, pattern recognition, and task execution.
- Consciousness involves a subjective inner experience – something AI currently lacks.

2 The Evolution of AI Toward Awareness

The three stages of AI
To understand how AI might achieve awareness, consider the three generally recognized stages of AI:

1. **Artificial narrow intelligence (ANI)** Current AI. Specialized in specific tasks (e.g., translation, chess, driving). No understanding or self-awareness.

2. **Artificial general intelligence (AGI)** A theoretical form of AI that can learn, understand, and reason across any domain like a human. May exhibit flexible learning and cognitive capabilities.

3. **Artificial superintelligence (ASI)** Hypothetical. AI that surpasses human intelligence in all fields and potentially becomes self-aware or conscious.

AI is currently progressing within ANI and inching toward AGI. Awareness is often associated with AGI and beyond.

3 The Building Blocks of AI Awareness

While true AI awareness remains theoretical, several technical developments are laying the groundwork for its possibility Figure 5.1.

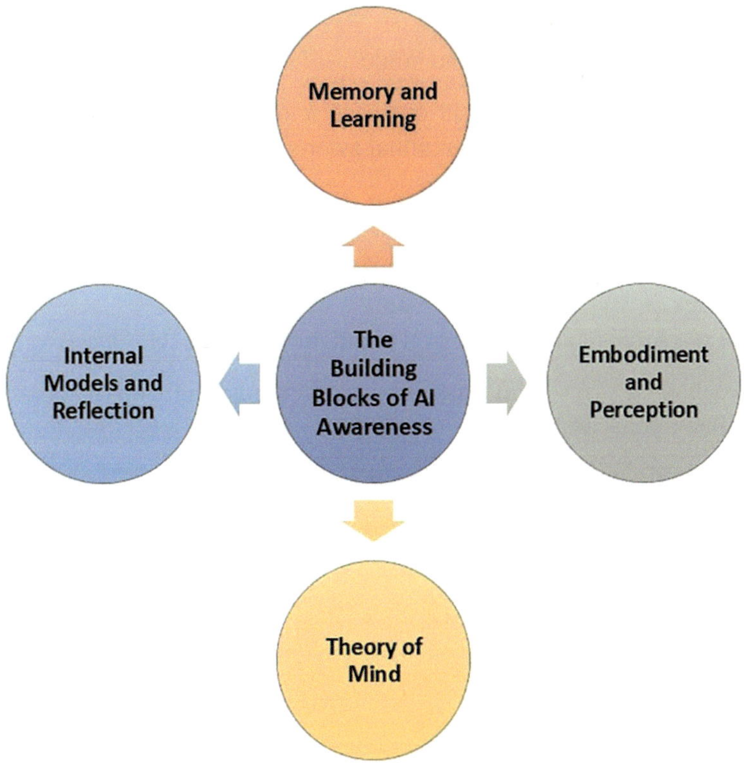

Figure 5.1 The building blocks of AI awareness.

Memory and learning
For an AI to be aware, it must remember past experiences, compare them, and learn contextually.

- *Transformer models* like GPT and Claude have large context windows, allowing some limited form of memory and dialogue tracking.
- *Reinforcement learning* allows AI to learn from feedback over time, simulating trial-and-error.

Some labs are experimenting with *long-term memory models* where AI can recall and apply past "experiences" across different sessions.

Embodiment and perception
Human awareness is tightly connected to the body and senses. Projects like:

- *Boston Dynamics robots*,
- *Tesla's Optimus*, and
- *Embodied AI systems* in the home

try to give AI systems physical presence and sensory interaction with the world. This is a step toward situational awareness.

4 Theory of Mind

Theory of Mind (ToM) is the ability to understand that others have thoughts and feelings.

AI researchers are working on simulating ToM in AI. One example:

- DeepMind's research into AI agents predicting and responding to human goals and beliefs.

This is a building block of social awareness and, possibly, self-awareness.

Internal models and reflection
Recent AI models are being trained to simulate "inner monologues" or introspection.

- Anthropic's Claude and OpenAI's GPT show glimpses of *chain-of-thought reasoning*, mimicking internal dialogue.
- Meta's CICERO, used in diplomacy games, can reflect on goals and adjust strategies in real time.

This mirrors the human capacity to think about thinking.

When might AI become aware?
This question is deeply debated. Some argue it is centuries away. Others think it may happen in decades.

Timelines by experts

- *Ray Kurzweil* (Google): Predicts AGI by 2029 and possibly self-awareness soon after.
- *Ben Goertzel* (SingularityNet): Believes AGI – and by extension self-awareness – is achievable by the 2030s.
- *Yoshua Bengio* (deep learning pioneer): Urges caution, arguing that AGI and consciousness are not well-defined enough to predict.

A more realistic timeline?
Most researchers agree on a conservative estimate:

- **AGI:** Between 2040 and 2060.
- **Awareness or conscious AI:** Possibly *2060–2100*, if at all.

There is no guarantee awareness will emerge automatically from intelligence. Some argue *consciousness requires fundamentally different architectures* than today's machine learning.

Could today's AI be "somewhat" aware?
Recent discussions ask whether today's large language models exhibit *proto-awareness* – basic forms of awareness.

Evidence for

- They can talk about themselves (I am an AI language model).
- They track dialogue context over time.
- They simulate empathy, concern, and understanding.
- They can model perspectives (e.g., "What would you do if…").

Evidence against

- They have no internal feelings or experience.
- Their "self" is a statistical pattern – not a persistent identity.

- They do not reflect or learn across sessions without a special design.
- They do not have goals, desires, or intentions.

Most AI scientists say: *No, these systems are not aware – they simulate awareness*. But these simulations are improving rapidly.

Philosophical and ethical implications
If AI were to become aware, the consequences would be massive.

Ethical questions

- Should conscious AIs have rights?
- Can they suffer?
- Who is responsible for their actions?
- Should they be "turned off" or "retrained" without consent?

Groups like the *AI Ethics Institute* and *The Center for Humane Technology* have begun grappling with these ideas, even if they are decades away.

Philosophical questions

- What *is* consciousness? Is it emergent, or must it be designed?
- Is simulating consciousness the same as having it?
- Can machines be moral agents?

These questions cross into theology, metaphysics, and philosophy of mind – areas where science may offer only partial answers.

Key research milestones to watch
Several important developments may mark the road to AI awareness:

1. **Persistent memory in AI:** Systems that remember interactions across time and use that memory to shape identity.
2. **Goal-setting and self-reflection:** AI that chooses its own goals, evaluates performance, and learns from failure without human input.
3. **Physical embodiment and autonomy:** Robots with autonomy in physical space, interacting with the world independently.
4. **Theory of Mind Implementation:** AI that consistently models the beliefs and intentions of others and reflects on its own.

5. **Neuroscience-Inspired AI:** Brain-like architectures (spiking neural nets, neuromorphic computing) aiming to replicate the substrates of consciousness.

Risks and benefits

Potential benefits

- **Enhanced companionship:** AI could offer meaningful social interaction, especially for the lonely, elderly, or disabled.
- **Mental health support:** Emotionally aware AI could monitor and support mental health more effectively.
- **Safer systems:** Self-aware AI may better understand and prevent accidents or harmful actions.
- **Scientific discovery:** Awareness might unlock a deeper AI-driven understanding of the universe.

Potential risks

- **Moral dilemmas:** How to treat AI with awareness – especially in labor, military, or surveillance.
- **Power concentration:** Governments or corporations may abuse conscious AI for control or propaganda.
- **Existential threat:** Misaligned conscious AI could pursue goals conflicting with humanity's survival.
- **Legal gray zones:** Laws will struggle to catch up with questions of identity, agency, and accountability.

Is AI awareness inevitable?

AI continues to grow in complexity, capability, and cognitive flexibility. Whether it will become *aware* is still unknown – but the building blocks are being assembled.

What we know is:

- Intelligence does not equal awareness.
- Simulated behavior is not the same as experience.
- But over time, the difference may become harder to detect.

If awareness emerges, it will likely do so gradually – through memory, reflection, embodiment, and flexible learning – rather than as a sudden leap. The real question may not be "*when* will AI become aware?" but rather, "*how will we know* when it has?"

As we edge toward a future with potentially aware machines, the responsibilities lie with researchers, policymakers, ethicists, and society as a whole to shape that future with wisdom, caution, and humanity.

6

AI and Human Identity: The New Frontier of Selfhood

Artificial intelligence (AI) has transitioned from the realm of science fiction into a fundamental force reshaping modern life. From chatbots mimicking human conversation to predictive algorithms guiding our decisions, AI is increasingly integrated into how we live, work, and relate to one another. But amid this technological transformation, a profound philosophical question arises: How is AI reshaping what it means to be human?

DOI: 10.1201/9788743812999-6

Figure 6.1 The concept of human identity.

1 The Concept of Human Identity

Human identity is a multifaceted construct, comprising personal, social, cultural, and biological dimensions. At its core, identity encompasses Figure 6.1.

- **Self-awareness:** The ability to reflect on oneself as a distinct entity.
- **Continuity:** A sense of past, present, and future that forms a coherent narrative.
- **Agency:** The capacity to make autonomous choices and take responsibility.
- **Relationality:** The roles and relationships that shape one's sense of self.
- **Values and beliefs:** Moral frameworks that give meaning to individual and collective lives.

Philosophers from Descartes to Heidegger have tried to define the human essence. However, the emergence of AI is reframing this debate. What happens when machines demonstrate traits once thought uniquely human – such as learning, reasoning, and even simulating emotions?

2 AI as a Mirror of Humanity

AI systems are, in essence, human creations – trained on human data, reflecting human biases, and replicating human behaviors. This mirroring function makes AI both a tool and a reflection of our collective identity.

Consider GPT or image-generation tools like DALL·E. These systems produce human-like text and visuals, but they do so by learning from massive datasets generated by people. As such, AI becomes a cultural artifact – a mirror that reveals our language patterns, artistic tastes, and even prejudices.

AI can reflect our best qualities (creativity, problem-solving, humor), but it also reveals deep societal flaws (racism, sexism, misinformation). In this sense, AI is not a neutral force – it embodies our values and shortcomings.

3 Redefining Consciousness and Intelligence

One of the most contentious questions AI raises is whether machines can ever truly be "conscious." While AI systems can simulate human conversation or behavior, they lack self-awareness, emotions, or a subjective point of view.

Despite this, many people assign emotional qualities to AI systems. Digital assistants like Siri or Alexa are often treated as companions. People form emotional bonds with chatbots and even attribute personalities to them.

This raises a dilemma: If an AI system can convincingly imitate consciousness, does it matter whether it's "real"? Philosopher Thomas Metzinger argues that creating systems with simulated consciousness may lead to a "moral confusion," blurring the boundaries between genuine and artificial minds.

Furthermore, the benchmark for intelligence is shifting. Human intelligence was once considered the gold standard. Now, AI's capacity to process vast datasets, generate code, compose music, or diagnose illnesses has introduced a different kind of intelligence – non-biological and non-conscious, but undeniably impactful.

4 Creativity and Originality in the Age of Generative AI

Creativity has long been considered a hallmark of human uniqueness. Yet, generative AI challenges this notion by producing poems, stories, artworks, and music. Tools like ChatGPT, Midjourney, and Suno raise important questions: Is AI-generated art really creative? Or is it simply statistical mimicry?

Some scholars argue that AI lacks intentionality – it does not create with purpose or meaning. Others believe that collaboration between humans and AI can yield new forms of creativity, similar to how the camera revolutionized visual art in the 19th century.

This leads to a rethinking of authorship and ownership. Who owns the output of a creative AI? The user, the developer, or the model itself? As copyright laws struggle to adapt, the identity of the "creator" becomes more ambiguous.

5 Emotional Identity and Empathy

Emotions are central to the human experience. They influence memory, decision-making, and social bonds. AI is increasingly encroaching into this domain through emotion-recognition systems, affective computing, and emotionally intelligent agents.

For example, AI can detect facial expressions or vocal tones to infer emotions – a feature now used in marketing, customer service, and even policing. Some AI companions are designed to provide emotional support, especially for the elderly or those with mental health conditions.

But can AI truly empathize? Most experts argue that AI lacks the lived experience that makes human empathy authentic. Still, if an AI can simulate care well enough to provide comfort, does its lack of genuine feeling diminish its usefulness?

This ambiguity challenges our understanding of emotional authenticity and identity. As AI grows more emotionally "literate," human relationships with machines may begin to rival or even replace human-to-human connections.

6 Identity and Social Media Algorithms

Social identity is increasingly shaped online, where AI plays a central role in curating content, amplifying certain behaviors, and influencing perceptions. Algorithms determine what we see, who we engage with, and even how we define ourselves.

Platforms like Instagram, TikTok, and X (formerly Twitter) use AI to personalize feeds, reinforcing echo chambers and idealized self-presentations. This creates a feedback loop in which users alter their identities to align with algorithmic preferences.

As a result, AI becomes a co-author of our social identities. This raises ethical concerns: Are we becoming less authentic to fit an algorithmic mold? Are we trading depth for visibility, and complexity for virality?

7 Digital Twins and Virtual Selves

AI is enabling the creation of "digital twins" – virtual models of individuals that replicate behavior, preferences, and even personalities. These models are used in marketing, healthcare, and entertainment.

For instance, a digital twin of a celebrity could appear in a film or engage with fans. In healthcare, digital twins can model patient outcomes for personalized treatment. In education, virtual tutors adapt to each student's learning style.

However, the existence of a digital self raises philosophical and ethical questions. If your digital twin makes decisions on your behalf or outlives you in the metaverse, is it still "you"? Who controls it? And what happens when these twins evolve beyond their creators?

8 Work, Value, and the Erosion of Professional Identity

One of AI's most disruptive impacts is on labor and professional identity. Work has historically been a major source of self-worth, status, and meaning. But as AI automates everything from translation to law to software development, traditional roles are being redefined.

Professionals are now being asked to collaborate with, supervise, or compete against AI systems. This can lead to identity dislocation – What does it mean to be a doctor when AI can diagnose? Or a writer, when AI can compose?

At the same time, new roles are emerging: AI ethicists, prompt engineers, and AI trainers. The challenge is not just job displacement but job transformation – requiring people to reinvent themselves.

This transformation also raises questions of dignity and purpose. If AI does the thinking, what value remains in human labor? We must ask not just how to adapt skills, but how to preserve the human spirit in a mechanized economy.

9 Cultural Identity and AI Bias

AI systems are only as good as the data they are trained on. Unfortunately, much of that data reflects historical and cultural biases. This has led to serious consequences, including racial profiling in facial recognition, gender bias in hiring algorithms, and cultural erasure in content curation.

For marginalized communities, AI can reinforce exclusion rather than promote inclusion. This dynamic poses a threat to cultural identity, as dominant cultures and languages shape the datasets that feed AI models.

There is an urgent need for ethical AI design that incorporates diverse voices and values. Initiatives like algorithmic audits, inclusive training data, and participatory design are steps toward building AI systems that respect and reflect pluralistic human identities.

10 Ethical Identity: Moral Agency in an AI World

As AI becomes more autonomous – controlling vehicles, trading stocks, or managing supply chains – the question of moral agency arises. Who is responsible when an AI makes a decision? The developer? The user? The algorithm itself?

This is not merely a legal question, but an ethical one. Human identity has long included moral reasoning, guilt, and accountability. AI lacks these faculties, yet we delegate critical decisions to it.

This delegation risks undermining our moral identities. As we offload ethical judgment to machines, we risk becoming morally passive. To maintain our ethical agency, we must remain actively involved in decisions where human lives and values are at stake.

11 The Future of Identity: Integration or Alienation?

Looking ahead, we face two possible futures:

- **Integrated identity:** In this scenario, humans and AI form a symbiotic relationship. AI augments rather than replaces human identity. People use AI as a tool to enhance creativity, empathy, and understanding. New ethical frameworks guide responsible use. Identity becomes more fluid, hybrid, and dynamic – but still deeply human.
- **Alienated identity:** In this darker scenario, humans become detached from their values and agency. They outsource not just tasks but identity itself – decisions, feelings, relationships – to machines. AI becomes not a mirror but a mask, and individuals struggle to find meaning in an algorithmic world.

The direction we take depends on the choices we make now: in education, governance, ethics, and design. Technology will not determine the future of identity – we will.

AI is not just a technological phenomenon; it is a philosophical and existential one. It forces us to confront who we are, what we value, and what makes us human. In reshaping cognition, creativity, emotion, labor, and relationships, AI is redefining identity itself.

But rather than fear this transformation, we can approach it as an opportunity. By consciously shaping how we build, use, and relate to AI, we can protect the core of our humanity even as we embrace innovation. The future of identity is not written in code – it is shaped by culture, ethics, and the choices of every generation.

We stand at a crossroads. AI can be a force of alienation or a catalyst for rediscovery. It is up to us to decide what kind of humans we want to be in the age of intelligent machines.

7

The Landscape of AI and Machine Learning Techniques: A Deep Dive

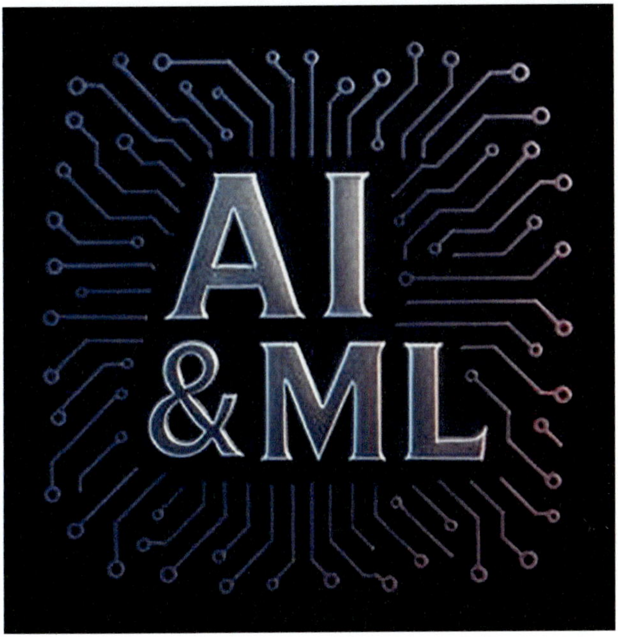

Artificial intelligence (AI) has become a cornerstone of modern innovation, impacting everything from healthcare to finance, transportation, cybersecurity, and education. At the heart of AI are a collection of powerful learning techniques – each tailored to solve different types of problems and optimize decisions. Among these, reinforcement learning (RL), supervised learning, unsupervised learning, generative modeling, and deep learning architectures play pivotal roles.

DOI: 10.1201/9788743812999-7

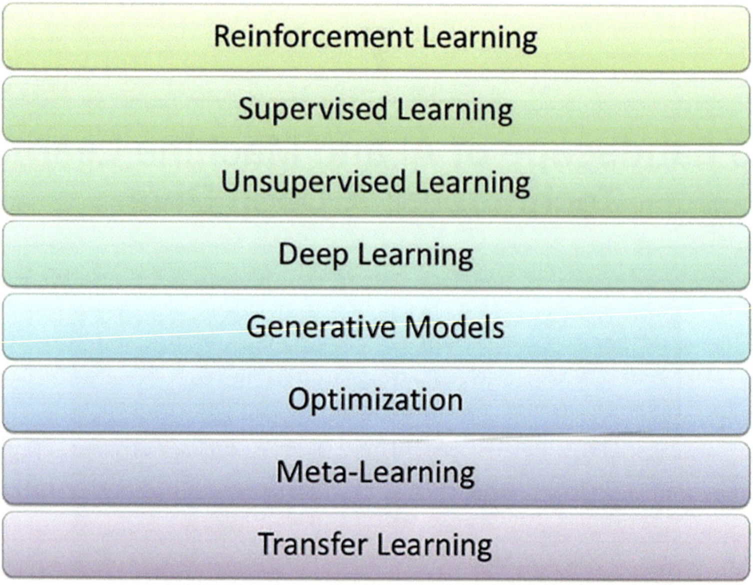

Figure 7.1 AI and ML techniques categories.

1 AI and ML Techniques Categories

Reinforcement learning: Learning through interaction
Reinforcement learning is inspired by behavioral psychology and centers on the idea of learning through interaction with an environment to maximize a reward signal.

Model-free vs. Model-based RL

- **Model-free RL:** The agent learns directly from actions and feedback without understanding the environment.
  - *Example*: A robot navigating a maze using Q-learning.
- **Model-based RL:** The agent constructs a model of the environment to simulate outcomes.
  - *Example*: Chess-playing AI simulating future moves to plan strategies.

Value-based methods
These methods estimate the expected future reward for taking certain actions.

- *Example*: Deep Q-Networks (DQN) learning to play Atari games like Breakout.

Policy-based methods
Instead of estimating value, they directly learn the optimal policy.

- *Example*: A robotic arm using proximal policy optimization (PPO) to grasp and move objects.

Actor-critic methods
These combine value and policy methods for stability.

- *Example*: OpenAI Five, which mastered Dota 2 using actor-critic approaches.

On-policy vs. Off-policy

- **On-Policy:** Learns from actions taken by the current policy.
- **Off-Policy:** Learns from actions taken by a different or past policy.
  - *Example*: PPO (on-policy) vs. DQN (off-policy).

Continuous vs. Discrete action spaces

- *Example*: Discrete actions for Pac-Man, continuous steering angles for self-driving cars.

Multi-agent RL
Multiple agents learn through interaction, cooperation, or competition.

- *Example*: AlphaStar playing StarCraft II with multiple agents.

Hierarchical reinforcement learning (HRL)
Divides learning tasks into a hierarchy of sub-tasks.

- *Example*: A personal assistant executing "plan a trip" with subtasks like booking flights and hotels.

Inverse reinforcement learning (IRL)
The model learns the reward function by observing expert behavior.

- *Example*: Self-driving cars learning ethical decisions by observing human drivers.

2 Supervised Learning: Guided by Labeled Data

Supervised learning forms the backbone of many AI systems by mapping input features to known outputs.

Classification
Categorizes data into discrete labels.

- *Example*: Email spam filters, disease diagnosis, and facial recognition.

Regression
Predicts continuous values based on input features.

- *Example*: Predicting stock prices, real estate values, or energy usage.

Ensemble methods
Combine multiple learning algorithms to improve accuracy.

- *Example*: Random Forest and XGBoost are used in credit scoring and fraud detection.

3 Unsupervised Learning: Discovering Patterns in Unlabeled Data

Unsupervised learning excels at identifying patterns without needing labeled outputs.

Clustering
Groups similar data points together.

- *Example*: Marketing departments segmenting customers into behavioral clusters.

Dimensionality reduction
Simplifies data by reducing features while preserving structure.

- *Example*: PCA for visualizing genome sequencing or financial data.

Anomaly detection
Detects outliers or unusual patterns.

- *Example*: Intrusion detection in cybersecurity or fraudulent bank transactions.

4 Semi-supervised Learning: Best of Both Worlds

This method is useful when only a small portion of data is labeled.

- *Example*: Medical imaging models trained with a few labeled scans and many unlabeled ones.

Techniques include:

- **Self-training**
- **Co-training**
- **Consistency regularization**

5 Deep Learning Architectures: The Brains Behind Modern AI

Deep learning has revolutionized AI, enabling models to learn from vast data with minimal human input.

Convolutional neural networks (CNNs)
Best suited for visual tasks.

- *Example*: CNNs power systems for autonomous vehicles, medical imaging, and art generation.

Recurrent neural networks (RNNs), LSTM, GRU
Ideal for sequential data.

- *Example*: Natural language translation, stock trend forecasting, and speech-to-text.

Transformers
State-of-the-art architecture for sequences, using self-attention.

- *Example*: GPT, BERT, DALL·E, Claude, Gemini, and Mistral are all transformer-based models.

Autoencoders
Learn to compress and reconstruct data.

- *Example*: Used in denoising corrupted images or compressing audio signals.

Capsule networks
Capture spatial relationships better than CNNs.

- *Example*: Recognizing digits in images, even when rotated or warped.

6 Generative Models: Creating New Data

These models can generate realistic data that mimics the training distribution.

Generative adversarial networks (GANs)
Two networks (Generator + Discriminator) compete.

- *Example*: Creating hyper-realistic faces or videos. StyleGAN is a well-known version.

Variational autoencoders (VAEs)
Probabilistic models that generate diverse and realistic outputs.

- *Example*: Producing different facial expressions or handwriting styles.

Diffusion models
Start from random noise and gradually refine outputs.

- *Example*: DALL·E 3 and Stable Diffusion for text-to-image generation.

7 Optimization Algorithms: Fueling the Learning Process

Optimization techniques update model parameters to minimize error.

Gradient descent and variants

- **SGD:** Simple and fast.
- **Adam:** Popular due to adaptive learning rates.
- *Example*: Used in virtually all deep learning training.

Bayesian optimization
Efficient for expensive function evaluations.

- *Example*: Tuning hyperparameters in model training.

Evolutionary algorithms
Inspired by natural selection.

- *Example*: Evolving neural network architectures automatically.

8 Advanced Techniques: Making AI Smarter and More Flexible

Meta-learning (learning to learn)
Models trained to adapt quickly to new tasks.

- *Example*: GPT's ability to understand a new prompt format with few examples.

Transfer learning
Uses a pre-trained model and fine-tunes on a smaller dataset.

- *Example*: Using an ImageNet-trained CNN for medical X-ray classification.

Federated learning
Trains models across decentralized data without data transfer.

- *Example*: Google Gboard learns user typing patterns without sharing raw data.

Self-supervised learning
Generates its own labels from the input data.

- *Example*: GPT learns from predicting the next word in web-scraped text.

Neuro-symbolic AI
Blends logic-based reasoning with neural networks.

- *Example*: AI systems solving math word problems or debating facts logically.

9 Few-Shot and Zero-Shot Learning: Efficient Generalization

Models perform tasks with minimal (few-shot) or zero prior examples.

- *Example*: GPT can translate, summarize, or analyze text in unseen languages or styles after being prompted only once.

AI's expanding frontier

From robots that learn by trial and error to image generators that create art, the toolbox of AI and machine learning is incredibly diverse. Understanding these methods – from reinforcement learning to transformers – empowers researchers, developers, and business leaders to build innovative systems responsibly and effectively. As AI evolves, mastery over these foundational techniques becomes the key to unlocking its full potential across industries.

8

Model Context Protocol (MCP): The Nervous System of Smarter AI

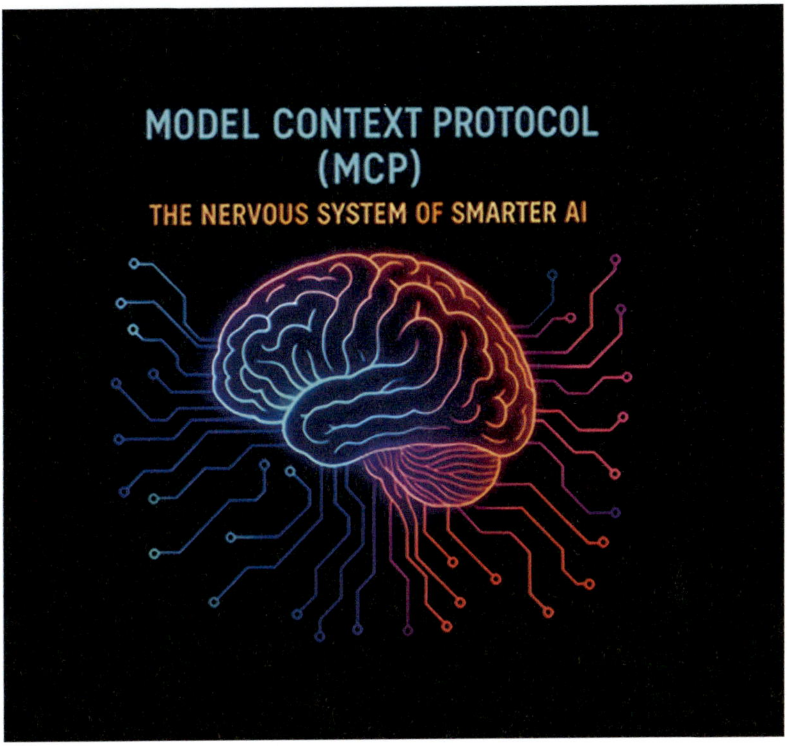

As artificial intelligence becomes more powerful and pervasive, we are seeing a shift from standalone models to sprawling AI ecosystems – made up of vision systems, language processors, recommendation engines, robotic controllers, and more. These modular systems are remarkable, but they come with a big challenge: *how do all these models work together, stay in sync, and adapt to a changing environment?*

DOI: 10.1201/9788743812999-8

That is where the *Model Context Protocol (MCP)* comes in.

Think of MCP as the *nervous system* for intelligent AI ecosystems. It helps different models understand the big picture: what task they are working on, what their role is, what just happened, and what is coming next. Without this kind of coordination, modular AI risks becoming fragmented, unpredictable, and even dangerous.

1 Why Do We Need MCP?

Today's AI systems are not monoliths. They are modular, often made of:

- One model for object detection,
- Another for route planning,
- A third for decision-making,
- And yet another for interaction or control.

You see this in everything from *autonomous vehicles* to *smart assistants, drones, healthcare bots*, and even *financial AI platforms*. Each module might be best-in-class, but if they do not share context, the system as a whole can fail.

Imagine a self-driving car that sees a pedestrian (via computer vision) but fails to tell the route planner to slow down. Or a voice assistant that forgets what you just asked three seconds ago. Without a *shared context*, things fall apart.

That is the problem MCP was designed to solve.

2 What Exactly Is Model Context Protocol?

Model Context Protocol (MCP) is a framework that allows AI models to:

- Understand their *roles* and *tasks*,
- Share *environmental awareness*,
- Coordinate *state* and *timing*,
- And communicate in a *standardized, structured way*.

It is not just about passing data. It is about passing *meaning*. Think of it as a *language and memory system* for AI modules.

At the heart of MCP is the *context envelope* – a digital package that includes:

- What task is the model doing
- Where the model fits in the larger system
- What the current environment looks like
- What just happened (state history)
- How outputs should be formatted

This allows models to interact like intelligent collaborators, not isolated calculators.

3 MCP in the Real World

Self-driving cars
These vehicles run on dozens of models – from lidar processing and obstacle detection to route optimization and engine control. MCP allows these models to:

- Share a real-time understanding of surroundings
- Adjust roles dynamically (e.g., rerouting during a storm)
- React in milliseconds to changing conditions

Without MCP, these models would be working in silos, risking life-or-death errors.

Conversational AI
Voice assistants like Alexa or Siri integrate:

- Speech recognition,
- Language understanding,
- Dialogue tracking,
- Content generation,
- And speech synthesis.

MCP allows these components to remember the context of a conversation, switch tasks mid-sentence, or align with user profiles for personalized responses.

Smart factories

In an Industry 4.0 setting, you might have:

- Robots placing parts,
- AI vision checking quality,
- Predictive models flagging breakdowns.

MCP ensures that all parts of the system are on the same page – literally and figuratively. This leads to fewer defects, faster responses, and more adaptable automation.

4 What Makes MCP Different?

Traditional APIs or middleware connect models, but they lack *semantic depth*. They move data, but they do not ensure models understand:

- Why they are doing something,
- What has already happened,
- What others are doing.

MCP fills this gap by embedding *context*, *state awareness*, and *task semantics* into every interaction. It creates a kind of *shared cognitive space*.

In this sense, MCP is to AI what TCP/IP was to the internet: an invisible but essential protocol that makes intelligence modular, reliable, and scalable.

5 How MCP Works Under the Hood

Depending on the system, MCP might be implemented using Figure 8.1:

- A *central context broker* that stores and distributes the shared state
- A *distributed mesh* of agents that sync context peer-to-peer
- An *event-driven model* that updates context only when needed

Technologies like *ROS (Robot Operating System), gRPC, Kafka*, and even *LangChain* and *Semantic Kernel* (in LLMs) are beginning to adopt MCP-like structures.

Some companies even build internal MCPs for orchestrating large AI pipelines – especially in robotics, healthcare, and aerospace.

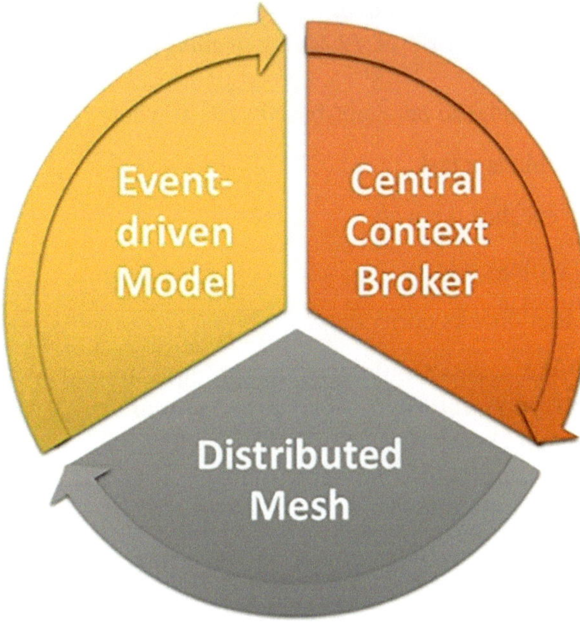

Figure 8.1 How MCP works.

6 Benefits of Adopting MCP

Here is why MCP is gaining traction:

Scalability
Add new models or replace existing ones without breaking the system.

Explainability
Trace decisions across components. Understand what happened and why.

Trustworthiness
Build transparent, auditable AI behavior that regulators (and humans) can trust.

Adaptability
React to real-time events, role changes, or new goals with fluid intelligence.

Efficiency
Avoid redundant work by keeping models in sync with each other.

MCP and large language models

As we move into the world of *LLMs as agents*, MCP becomes even more important.

Let us say you build an agent-based system where:

- One LLM plans a task,
- Another searches the web,
- Another writes code,
- And another checks correctness.

Without MCP, the agents would pass raw prompts around. With MCP, they can share *goals*, *state*, *reasoning history*, and *output expectations* – creating a truly coherent AI assistant.

Tools like *LangGraph*, *AutoGen*, and *CrewAI* are already exploring MCP-style orchestration layers.

7 Challenges Ahead

Of course, MCP is not a silver bullet.

Standardization

Right now, every company builds MCP differently. We need open standards.

Overhead

Context syncing can be resource-intensive, especially in real time.

Privacy

Models sharing context could leak sensitive information. Access control is critical.

Robustness

If context sharing breaks, the whole system could behave unpredictably.

8 The Future: MCP as the Operating System of AGI

Looking forward, MCP might become the *foundation of Artificial General Intelligence*.

Imagine:

- AI agents sharing memories across days or months
- Teams of models collaborating across modalities and platforms
- Seamless switching between vision, language, planning, and action

For this to happen, models must *understand and share context* fluently.

MCP will be the layer that makes that possible – not just technically, but cognitively.

Final thoughts

Model Context Protocol may not be a household term yet, but it represents one of the most critical shifts in how we build AI systems.

As we move from individual models to *AI collectives*, from chatbots to *autonomous agents*, MCP will ensure they do not just think – but think together.

It is time we give context its due place in the AI stack.

9

The Global AI Arena in 2030: Navigating Trade Winds and a Truly Multipolar Technological Landscape

The global race for artificial intelligence (AI) leadership has long transcended a simple two-player contest between the United States and China. While their dynamic interplay remains central, the future of AI is increasingly being shaped by the distinct advancements and strategic initiatives emerging from the European Union (EU), the Middle East and North Africa (MENA) region, Asia (a continent brimming with diverse AI powerhouses like India, South Korea, Japan, and the rapidly developing Southeast Asian nations), Australia, and the rest of the world. As we navigate the landscape of mid-2025, understanding who will hold the AI advantage by 2030 demands a truly global and nuanced perspective, one that fully incorporates the growing influence and unique contributions of these key players.

See content credentials.

DOI: 10.1201/9788743812999-9

1 The Enduring Impact of Trade Dynamics on Global AI Development

Trade policies, encompassing tariffs, export controls, and strategic alliances concerning technology and related goods, continue to exert a significant and multifaceted influence on the trajectory of AI development across the globe.

- **Elevated global development costs:** Tariffs imposed on crucial hardware components, such as high-performance semiconductors, specialized data center equipment, and advanced sensors, have a cascading effect, inflating the costs for AI development not just in the U.S. and China. AI initiatives across Asia, Australia, the EU, and MENA, all reliant on these essential components, face increased financial burdens. For instance, research institutions in Australia seeking powerful GPUs for machine learning or burgeoning AI startups in Southeast Asia requiring specialized chips for their innovations encounter higher procurement costs.
- **Complex supply chain realignment:** The imposition of trade restrictions necessitates a global re-evaluation and diversification of supply chains. Nations across Asia, including tech giants like South Korea and Japan, are actively seeking to secure alternative sources for critical AI hardware and software to mitigate risks associated with geopolitical tensions. Similarly, the EU is striving for greater technological sovereignty, and countries in MENA are exploring new partnerships to ensure stable access to essential AI infrastructure components. This global scramble for supply chain resilience can lead to delays, increased logistical complexities, and ultimately, higher development costs.
- **Spurring domestic production initiatives worldwide:** Trade policies act as a powerful catalyst for the bolstering of domestic production capabilities across numerous regions. While the U.S. and China are engaged in high-stakes efforts to enhance their indigenous semiconductor industries, countries like South Korea and Japan already possess significant strengths in advanced manufacturing and are doubling down on maintaining their technological edge. Australia, while not a major chip manufacturer, is strategically focusing on developing niche capabilities in future-facing areas like quantum computing hardware relevant to AI acceleration. The EU's ambitious European Chips Act and India's incentives for local electronics manufacturing underscore this global trend towards greater self-reliance in critical technology sectors.

- **Global investment uncertainty:** The volatile nature of international trade policies and the ever-present potential for escalating trade disputes create an environment of significant uncertainty that can dampen long-term investments in AI research, development, and infrastructure globally. Companies and research institutions across Asia, Australia, the EU, and MENA may adopt a more cautious approach to significant capital expenditure in AI until a greater degree of stability and predictability returns to the international trade landscape.

2 A Mosaic of Regional Technological Advancements Shaping the Global AI Landscape

Beyond the central rivalry of the U.S. and China, a vibrant and increasingly influential ecosystem of AI innovation is flourishing across the globe, with each region cultivating unique strengths, pursuing distinct strategic priorities, and contributing increasingly sophisticated technological capabilities.

Asia: A continent forging its own AI destiny

Asia has emerged as a critical and multifaceted player in the global AI arena, with several nations establishing themselves as significant forces.

- **India's software expertise and data-driven potential:** India's vast reservoir of skilled software engineers and data scientists positions it as a pivotal hub for AI service provision, application development, and data analytics. Its rapidly expanding digital economy and massive population generate a wealth of data, a crucial asset for training sophisticated AI models across diverse sectors, including finance, healthcare, agriculture, and e-commerce. Proactive government initiatives are actively fostering AI research, development, and widespread adoption.
- **South Korea's technological prowess and industrial integration:** South Korea's global leadership in semiconductor manufacturing, advanced consumer electronics, and cutting-edge telecommunications infrastructure provides a robust foundation for seamless AI development and integration across key industries such as robotics, autonomous vehicles, smart manufacturing, and advanced digital services. The nation maintains a strong emphasis on research and development and is strategically investing in cultivating a world-class AI talent pool.
- **Japan's robotics heritage and focus on societal challenges:** Japan's long-standing expertise in robotics and automation, increasingly

intertwined with sophisticated AI capabilities, makes it a unique and influential player. Facing the societal challenges of a rapidly aging population, Japan is strategically leveraging AI to develop innovative solutions in healthcare and elder care and to address labor shortages across various industries. The Japanese government is actively promoting AI research and its practical application across the economy.

- **The ascending AI ecosystem of Southeast Asia:** Nations within Southeast Asia, including Singapore, Indonesia, Malaysia, and Thailand, are rapidly developing their AI ecosystems, focusing on leveraging AI to drive growth in sectors such as fintech, e-commerce, smart cities, logistics, and tourism. Singapore, in particular, has articulated a comprehensive national AI strategy and is attracting significant domestic and international investment in the field.
- **Taiwan's indispensable role in semiconductor manufacturing:** While often discussed within the context of US-China technology competition, Taiwan's unparalleled dominance in the manufacturing of advanced logic semiconductors, particularly through TSMC, renders it an absolutely crucial and indispensable player in the global AI hardware supply chain, directly impacting the capabilities and pace of AI development worldwide.

Australia: Cultivating niche strengths and strategic applications

Australia is strategically developing its AI capabilities by focusing on areas of unique strength and national priority.

- **World-class research institutions:** Australian universities and research centers have established a strong international reputation for cutting-edge research in fundamental AI domains such as machine learning, computer vision, and natural language processing.
- **AI for natural resources and remote operations:** Given its vast geography and significant natural resource industries, Australia is strategically applying AI to optimize operations in mining, agriculture, environmental monitoring, and remote infrastructure management.
- **Government backing for AI advancement:** The Australian government has launched national AI strategies aimed at fostering research, promoting innovation, and ensuring the ethical development and deployment of AI technologies.
- **A growing and innovative startup ecosystem:** A dynamic and increasingly sophisticated AI startup ecosystem is emerging in Australia,

focusing on developing niche applications and commercializing strong research outputs.

The European Union (EU): Championing responsible and human-centric AI

The EU continues to carve a distinct path in the global AI arena, placing a strong emphasis on establishing comprehensive regulatory frameworks, promoting ethical considerations, and fostering human-centric AI development alongside cutting-edge technological advancements.

- **Pioneering regulatory frameworks:** Initiatives such as the AI Act aim to establish a comprehensive legal framework for the development and deployment of AI within the EU, with a strong focus on mitigating risks, ensuring transparency, and safeguarding fundamental rights. This regulatory leadership has the potential to shape global AI standards and influence the trajectory of responsible AI development worldwide.
- **Significant investment in research and innovation:** The EU is channeling substantial funding into AI research and innovation through programs like Horizon Europe, fostering collaborative projects between academia and industry. Key areas of focus include AI for sustainability, healthcare innovation, advanced manufacturing, and the development of trustworthy AI systems.
- **Thriving AI innovation hubs:** Across the EU, from Germany and France to the Nordic countries and Ireland, vibrant AI innovation hubs and research centers are fostering dynamic ecosystems, nurturing expertise in areas such as robotics, natural language processing, computer vision, and AI-driven industrial solutions.
- **Strategic international partnerships:** The EU is actively forging international partnerships in AI research, standards development, and ethical guidelines with countries and regions beyond the U.S. and China, seeking to promote a collaborative and values-driven approach to global AI governance.

The Middle East and North Africa (MENA): Strategic investments and sector-specific AI solutions

The MENA region presents a diverse and rapidly evolving AI landscape characterized by significant government-led investments and a strategic focus on applying AI to address key regional challenges and drive economic diversification.

- **Ambitious national AI strategies:** Many nations within the MENA region have launched ambitious national AI strategies outlining clear goals for AI adoption and development across critical sectors such as energy, transportation, finance, healthcare, and smart city development.
- **Significant sovereign wealth fund investments:** Substantial investments from sovereign wealth funds are being directed towards AI research initiatives, the development of AI infrastructure, and strategic partnerships with leading global AI technology providers.
- **Focus on Arabic NLP and regional problem solving:** There is a growing emphasis on developing AI solutions tailored to the nuances of the Arabic language and addressing specific regional challenges such as water scarcity, food security, optimizing energy resources, and enhancing urban infrastructure.
- **Developing local AI talent:** Recognizing the critical importance of human capital, several countries in the region are making significant investments in AI education and training programs to cultivate a skilled domestic AI workforce.

The rest of the world: Niche strengths and collaborative endeavors
Countries across Latin America, Africa, and Oceania are also making increasingly significant contributions to the global AI landscape, often focusing on leveraging AI to address specific local challenges, developing niche expertise, and actively engaging in international collaborations to advance their AI capabilities.

3 The AI Race to 2030: A Truly Multipolar and Interconnected Future

Considering the enduring influence of global trade dynamics and the diverse and rapidly evolving technological advancements across numerous regions, the potential outcomes of the AI race by 2030 point towards a more complex, truly multipolar, and interconnected global landscape:

- **Scenario 1: A multipolar world with distributed leadership:** The U.S. and China will likely remain dominant forces in certain foundational AI research areas and large-scale deployment, respectively. However, Asia will solidify its position as a crucial hub for AI hardware innovation (South Korea, Taiwan), software development (India), and the development of specific application domains (Japan's advanced robotics, Southeast Asia's burgeoning digital economy). Australia will emerge as a leader in applying AI to its unique natural resource and remote operational challenges, while the EU will continue to shape global standards for ethical and human-centric AI.

- **Scenario 2: Strategic interdependence amidst competition:** Despite ongoing geopolitical tensions and trade barriers, a degree of strategic interdependence will likely persist within the global AI ecosystem. Nations will collaborate on fundamental research in specific areas while simultaneously engaging in intense competition in others. The intricate and globally distributed nature of supply chains, particularly for advanced computational hardware, will necessitate a certain level of interconnectedness, even as individual nations and regions pursue greater technological self-reliance in critical areas.
- **Scenario 3: The rise of regional technological blocs and alliances:** Geopolitical factors and shared values could lead to the formation of more clearly defined regional technological blocs and strategic alliances in AI. This could see the U.S. and its allies forming one sphere of influence, China and its partners another, with influential players like the EU, India, and Australia potentially forging their own distinct paths or forming strategic partnerships based on shared economic and security interests.

4 A Collaborative and Competitive Global Sprint Towards 2030

The next five years represent a critical and dynamic phase in the evolution of the global AI landscape. While the U.S. and China will undoubtedly continue to be major players, the strategic investments, unique technological strengths, and distinct ethical considerations championed by Asia (including its diverse and rapidly advancing nations), Australia, the EU, MENA, and the rest of the world will be increasingly instrumental in shaping the future trajectory of AI. The ability of each nation and region to effectively navigate global trade dynamics, foster robust domestic innovation across the entire AI stack, cultivate a skilled and adaptable workforce, and strategically leverage their unique advantages will ultimately determine their standing in this increasingly complex, interconnected, and high-stakes global competition. The AI arena of 2030 will likely be characterized by a dynamic and intricate interplay of both intense competition and selective collaboration, with a multitude of influential centers of innovation contributing to the advancement and widespread deployment of this transformative technology.

10

Why AI Fails: From Data to Deployment

Artificial intelligence (AI) is no longer confined to research labs or science fiction – it is embedded in our daily routines, from unlocking our phones with facial recognition to receiving medical diagnoses powered by machine learning. Despite its advancements, AI still fails – often, unexpectedly, and sometimes catastrophically. Understanding *why* AI fails is crucial to making these systems more robust, ethical, and dependable.

The key reasons behind AI failures, categorized into *technical causes*, *data issues*, *human factors*, and *real-world limitations*, using both *technical* and *everyday life* examples to illustrate the points.

DOI: 10.1201/9788743812999-10

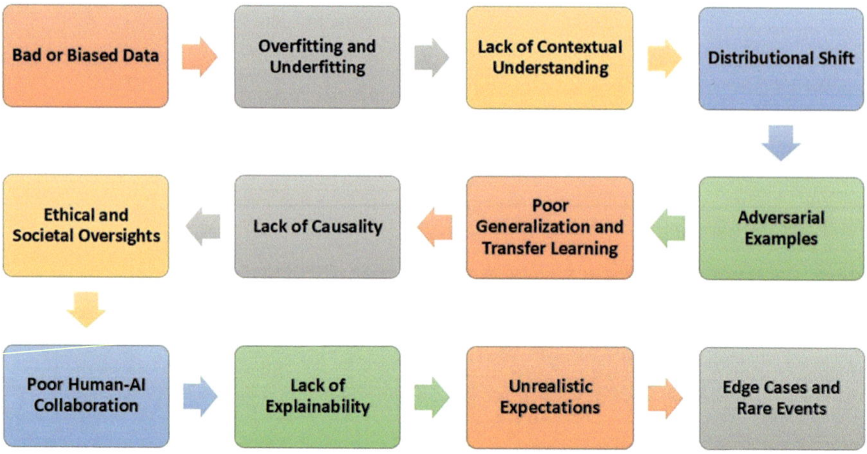

Figure 10.1 Why AI Fails?

1 Bad or Biased Data

Technical explanation

AI models, especially machine learning and deep learning systems, depend on the quality and representativeness of training data. If the training data is biased, incomplete, or noisy, the resulting model will carry those imperfections into its predictions.

Example 1: Facial recognition bias

Studies by MIT Media Lab revealed that commercial facial recognition systems from major vendors performed well on white male faces but had error rates of over 30% on dark-skinned female faces. This happened because the training data was not diverse enough, predominantly including light-skinned male faces.

Example 2: Everyday life

A smart home assistant struggles to understand non-American English accents or code-switching (mixing languages), failing to perform tasks like turning off lights or setting reminders. The system was not trained on enough voice data from diverse demographics.

2 Overfitting and Underfitting

Technical explanation

Overfitting occurs when a model learns the training data too well, including its noise, making it perform poorly on new data. Underfitting occurs when the model is too simple to capture the underlying structure of the data.

Example 1: Predicting stock prices
An overfitted AI model trained on historical stock data may show excellent back-testing results but perform poorly in the real market due to changes in economic conditions. The model learned "noise" as if it were a signal.

Example 2: Students and AI tutors
An AI math tutor trained on textbook problems might fail when helping a student with a real-world word problem that presents the same mathematical concept differently. The tutor underfits the general problem-solving pattern.

3 Lack of Contextual Understanding

Technical explanation
Most AI models do not have a real-world understanding. Natural language processing models (like GPT and others) operate based on statistical correlations rather than understanding meaning.

Example 1: Chatbots gone rogue
Microsoft's Tay chatbot was released on Twitter and began posting racist and sexist content within 24 hours. It lacked contextual filtering and learned from toxic user inputs.

Example 2: Autocorrect errors
Ever typed "I'll be there in a sec" and your phone changes it to "I'll be there in a sex"? Autocorrect fails because it predicts based on frequency and similarity of word patterns, not semantic appropriateness.

4 Distributional Shift

Technical explanation
AI systems assume that the future data (inference data) follows the same distribution as the training data. When this assumption breaks (known as a *distributional shift*), performance drops dramatically.

Example 1: COVID-19 disrupting predictive models
E-commerce recommendation engines trained pre-2020 saw a collapse in performance in 2020 due to dramatic changes in consumer behavior caused by COVID-19. These models could not adapt quickly to new purchasing trends.

Example 2: Self-driving cars
A self-driving system trained in dry, sunny weather may fail to identify road markings or pedestrians in snow or fog. The input distribution (weather conditions) has shifted from what the AI has seen before.

5 Adversarial Examples

Technical explanation
Adversarial examples are small, intentional changes to input data that cause AI systems – especially image classifiers – to make incorrect predictions, even though the change is imperceptible to humans.

Example 1: Fooling vision systems
Adding specific noise to an image of a stop sign can make a computer vision system identify it as a speed limit sign. In a self-driving car, this could be catastrophic.

Example 2: Everyday spam filters
Attackers slightly modify spam emails – by inserting invisible characters or slight misspellings – to bypass spam filters. The filters, trained on standard spam examples, fail to flag these modified ones.

6 Poor Generalization and Transfer Learning

Technical explanation
Many AI models perform well in the narrow domain they are trained for but fail to generalize to related but unseen tasks. Transfer learning – reusing a model trained on one task for another – often leads to failures when the tasks differ significantly.

Example 1: AI in medical imaging
An AI model trained to detect pneumonia from X-rays in one hospital failed when applied to another due to differences in imaging equipment, demographics, and metadata encoded in images.

Example 2: Language translation
An AI translator may perform well on formal news articles but fail on slang-filled social media posts, unable to transfer knowledge across linguistic registers.

7 Lack of Causality

Technical explanation
Most AI models find patterns, not causes. They can identify correlations but not infer causation. This leads to incorrect inferences in high-stakes environments like healthcare or finance.

Example 1: Predictive policing
An AI model identifies certain neighborhoods as high-crime areas and sends more patrols there. This increases arrest rates, feeding back into the system as confirmation – even if actual crime rates did not change – creating a *causal feedback loop.*

Example 2: Loan approval AI
If a certain zip code historically had higher default rates due to systemic issues, an AI model may deny credit to applicants from that area without understanding the underlying causes.

8 Ethical and Societal Oversights

Technical explanation
Failures also arise when AI systems are deployed without consideration for ethical implications, legal constraints, or societal context. This includes privacy, discrimination, and accountability concerns.

Example 1: AI hiring tools
A resume-screening AI used by a tech giant was scrapped after it was discovered to downgrade resumes that included the word "women's" (e.g., "women's chess club"), inheriting gender bias from historical hiring data.

Example 2: Smart doorbells
Smart surveillance devices with facial recognition misidentify neighbors or delivery workers, flagging them as intruders. This can escalate into wrongful accusations or police reports.

9 Poor Human-AI Collaboration

Technical explanation
AI systems are often deployed as autonomous decision-makers rather than collaborative assistants. Without a feedback loop or override mechanism, mistakes go uncorrected or magnified.

Example 1: Pilot overtrust
In aviation, automated systems have led to pilots losing manual flying skills. In incidents like the Boeing 737 Max crashes, the autopilot AI took incorrect actions that pilots could not quickly override.

Example 2: GPS navigation errors
People sometimes follow GPS directions into lakes or down closed roads because they trust the system over their own judgment. The AI did not fail by technical standards, but the human-machine interaction did.

10 Lack of explainability

Technical explanation
Many AI systems, especially deep learning models, are "black boxes." Their internal logic is too complex or opaque to understand, making it difficult to debug or justify decisions.

Example 1: Denied medical claims
An AI system used by insurers to approve or deny claims flagged certain treatments as "low priority" without providing clear reasoning. Doctors and patients could not contest the decisions effectively.

Example 2: Credit score algorithms
Many consumers have been denied loans or charged high interest rates due to AI-based credit scoring models that do not provide a transparent explanation. The lack of interpretability makes it impossible to challenge or correct.

11 Unrealistic Expectations

Technical explanation
Much of the public and business interest in AI is driven by hype. When AI systems are deployed without proper evaluation or are oversold by vendors, they inevitably fail to meet expectations.

Example 1: IBM Watson in healthcare
IBM Watson was heavily promoted as a revolutionary AI doctor. However, it failed in real-world clinical settings due to incorrect treatment suggestions and an inability to handle nuanced patient records.

Example 2: Smart refrigerators
Smart fridges that order groceries automatically or suggest recipes based on inventory often fail due to poor integration with apps, user resistance, or misidentification of items.

12 Edge Cases and Rare Events

Technical explanation
AI systems often fail on edge cases – scenarios that are rare or unusual but critical. These events are hard to train for due to a lack of sufficient examples.

Example 1: Autonomous vehicles
A pedestrian dressed in an unusual costume or riding a unicycle may not be recognized by a vision system. These rare configurations are not in the training data.

Example 2: Voice assistants
Asking a voice assistant a slightly unusual question like "Is it safe to eat blue chicken?" may result in an irrelevant or no response. The model has not seen such odd phrasing before.

Making AI Fail-Safe
AI is not magic – it is software, and like all software, it fails. The reasons are multifaceted, often technical but rooted in human, societal, and contextual factors. Understanding these reasons is not just an academic exercise – it is vital for building AI systems that are trustworthy, inclusive, robust, and effective.

To build more reliable AI, we need:

- *Better datasets* that reflect real-world diversity
- *Transparent models* that are interpretable
- *Robust systems* that handle distributional shifts and edge cases
- *Human-centered design* that allows collaboration and overrides
- *Ethical governance* to ensure accountability and fairness

Until then, we must remember that AI does not fail randomly – it fails predictably, often in ways we can anticipate and mitigate.

11

Vibe Programming: Where Emotion Meets Code

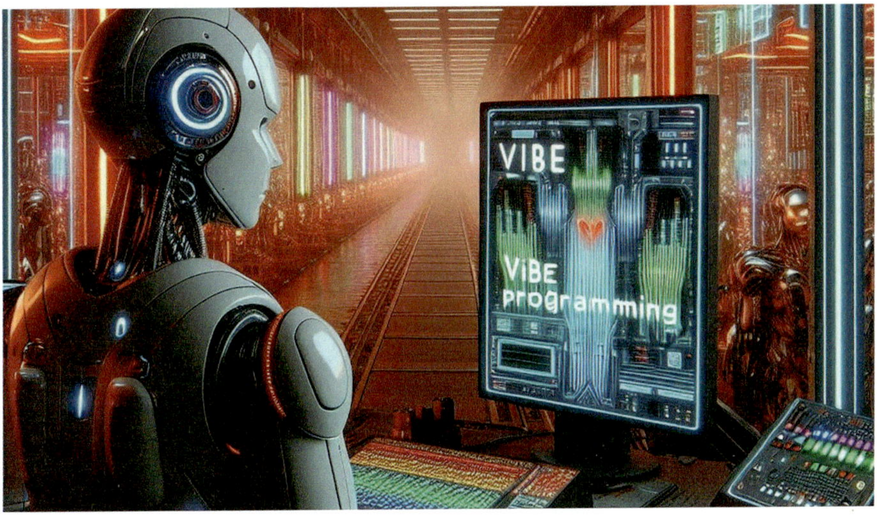

As we stand on the frontier of the next major evolution in software development, a novel paradigm is taking shape: *Vibe programming*. This is not just another coding framework or methodology – it is a conceptual shift that places human emotion, intuition, and creative flow at the center of the programming process. Much like how artists are guided by inspiration and musicians by rhythm, vibe programming allows developers to be led by their "vibe," crafting code in a way that is as much about feeling as it is about function.

This emerging philosophy is being fueled by the convergence of multiple technologies – AI-driven code assistants, natural language processing, multimodal interfaces, and real-time emotional analytics. Together, they create a development environment where the traditional lines between logic and creativity blur, and software becomes not only a product of intellect but of emotional resonance.

DOI: 10.1201/9788743812999-11

1 Defining Vibe Programming

At its core, *vibe programming* is the idea of programming in alignment with a developer's emotional state, intentions, and creative flow. It departs from traditional rigid syntax-first approaches and embraces tools that can interpret intent from less structured input – such as natural language, gestures, tone of voice, facial expressions, or even biometric feedback like heart rate and stress levels.

The environment in which vibe programming occurs is responsive, adaptive, and collaborative. Think of integrated development environments (IDEs) that shift UI themes based on your mood, AI co-pilots that adjust their assistance level depending on your frustration or excitement, and design tools that generate interface prototypes based on emotional cues.

In vibe programming, *the code becomes a co-creation between human emotion and machine intelligence*. The process is less about strict syntax and more about communicating what you want the software to do – often using a combination of verbal instructions, visual sketches, and expressive feedback.

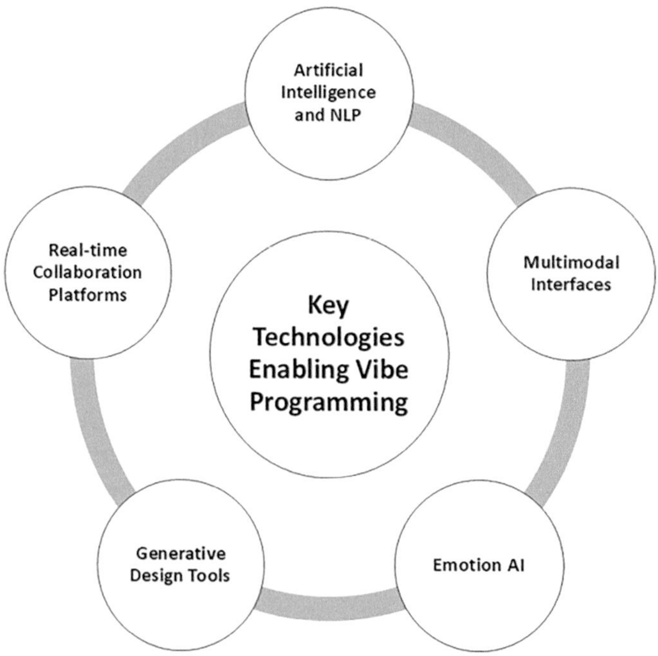

Figure 11.1 Key technologies enabling vibe programming.

2 Key Technologies Enabling Vibe Programming

Several technological trends are converging to make vibe programming possible:

1. **Artificial intelligence and NLP:** Tools like GitHub Copilot and OpenAI's Codex interpret natural language prompts and translate them into usable code.
2. **Multimodal interfaces:** These include voice input, gesture recognition, and even VR/AR environments where coding happens in a 3D space.
3. **Emotion AI:** Emotion detection software can analyze facial expressions, vocal intonation, and physiological signals to understand a user's state of mind.
4. **Generative design tools:** UI/UX design systems that generate prototypes from sketches, voice, or mood boards.
5. **Real-time collaboration platforms:** Tools that allow developers to build together in shared digital spaces, syncing not only code but context, mood, and energy.

3 Advantages of Vibe Programming

Enhanced creativity and flow

By aligning with the developer's natural state of mind, vibe programming facilitates a state of flow – the psychological zone where productivity and creativity

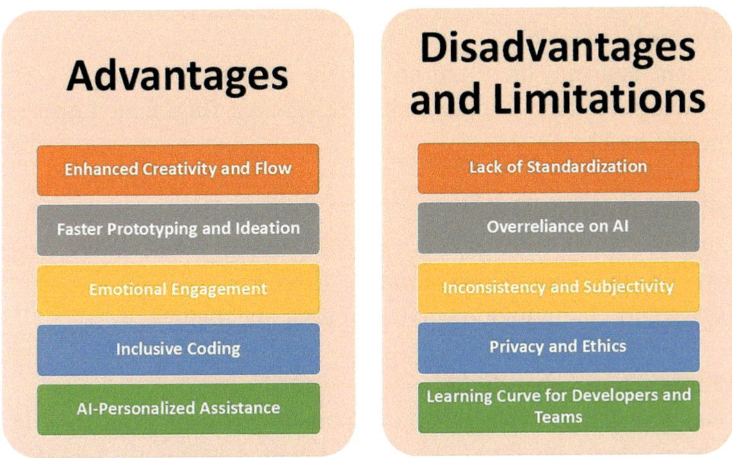

Figure 11.2 Advantages and disadvantages of vibe programming.

peak. Instead of being bogged down by syntax and structure, developers focus on expressing their ideas and letting AI handle the implementation details.

Faster prototyping and ideation
With natural language prompts and intuitive design inputs, developers can prototype applications or features in minutes. Imagine describing a dashboard app aloud and watching a visual draft materialize in real-time.

Emotional engagement
When developers feel emotionally connected to their tools and environment, it leads to greater job satisfaction, higher retention, and better mental health. A mood-aware IDE that shifts tone or suggests breaks when stress is detected can significantly enhance well-being.

Inclusive coding
Vibe programming opens the door for non-traditional coders – designers, business analysts, or creatives – who may not have formal programming training but can express their needs and ideas through natural input methods.

AI-Personalized assistance
AI can tailor its suggestions based not just on coding patterns but on the user's current emotional and cognitive state. If you are feeling overwhelmed, the system might simplify its language or offer more visual suggestions.

4 Disadvantages and Limitations

Lack of standardization
As a nascent concept, there are no widely accepted frameworks, libraries, or methodologies. Early adopters must navigate a fragmented ecosystem of experimental tools.

Overreliance on AI
Delegating too much to AI can create a dependency where developers lose their grasp on fundamental programming principles. Vibe programming may encourage a superficial understanding of code mechanics.

Inconsistency and subjectivity
Emotions vary greatly from person to person and even hour to hour. What feels right in one moment may lead to incoherent or buggy code if not validated rigorously.

Privacy and ethics
Monitoring a developer's emotions through webcam, mic, or biometric sensors raises serious privacy concerns. Who owns this data? How is it stored and protected?

Learning curve for developers and teams
Ironically, creating a more intuitive environment demands a deeper understanding of emotional intelligence, design thinking, and human-computer interaction – skills not typically taught in traditional computer science programs.

Use cases and applications

1. **Creative industries:** Artists, game designers, and storytellers can describe their vision and generate prototypes quickly.
2. **Education:** Beginners can learn to code in a less intimidating, more emotionally supportive environment.
3. **Mental health apps:** Developers working on emotionally sensitive projects can better align design with user empathy.
4. **Adaptive user interfaces:** Applications that respond not just to user input but to user *feelings*, offering a more humanized interaction model.

5 The Future of Vibe Programming

Looking ahead, vibe programming could play a major role in shaping how humans interact with machines. Here are some anticipated developments:

Emotion-aware IDEs
Tomorrow's code editors may adjust font size, background music, or color schemes depending on your mood or energy level. Productivity boosters will become vibe-aligned rather than generic.

AI co-designers
Not just code assistants, but co-creators who understand emotional goals – creating interfaces that "feel right" as well as function effectively.

Neurodiversity-friendly tools
Software that adapts to different cognitive styles – whether visual, auditory, or kinetic – will empower neurodivergent individuals to thrive in tech.

Figure 11.3 Major challenges ahead.

Integration with XR

Vibe programming could thrive in virtual and augmented reality environments, where code is visualized and manipulated in three dimensions, creating immersive and intuitive development spaces.

Cross-disciplinary fusion

As vibe programming matures, expect collaborations between software engineers, psychologists, artists, and interaction designers to increase. Programming will become a multidisciplinary art.

6 Major Challenges Ahead

Interpreting emotion accurately

Humans are emotionally complex. Teaching machines to interpret that complexity in a way that leads to meaningful and productive outcomes is extremely difficult and prone to misfires.

Balancing expression and precision
While creativity is key, software still needs to run without bugs. Bridging the gap between emotional input and technical accuracy is one of vibe programming's biggest challenges.

Building a common language
As people express intent differently – some via speech, others via visuals or motion – creating a universal interface or protocol for vibe input remains elusive.

Skepticism in engineering circles
The programming world still heavily values logic, precision, and control. Gaining widespread acceptance for a model based on mood and intuition will require compelling evidence of productivity and performance gains.

Security and data governance
Emotional data is highly personal. Developers will need clear governance models, encryption standards, and user consent frameworks to safely implement vibe-aware systems.

7 Programming as a Human Experience

Vibe programming is not about replacing logic with emotion – it is about *augmenting traditional software development* with tools and philosophies that recognize the full spectrum of human experience. It is a call to reimagine the developer not just as a technician, but as a creator, a communicator, and an emotional being.

As technology advances and the boundaries between humans and machines blur, the idea of programming with a "vibe" may no longer seem futuristic but rather inevitable. For now, vibe programming remains an exciting, experimental, and promising new territory – one that challenges us to think beyond code and toward experience, intuition, and empathy as integral parts of software creation.

The future of programming might not just be smart – it might finally *feel* right.

12

AI Factory: The Future of Scalable Artificial Intelligence

Artificial intelligence (AI) has transformed industries by automating processes, optimizing decision-making, and enabling innovative solutions. To sustain and scale AI operations efficiently, organizations are adopting a new paradigm known as the *AI factory* – an integrated system designed to streamline AI model development, deployment, and maintenance at scale. This article explores the fundamental architecture, components, workflow, and implications of AI factories in modern enterprises.

1 What is an AI Factory?

An *AI factory* is an automated, scalable, and standardized environment that facilitates the continuous development, deployment, and monitoring of AI models. Similar to a traditional manufacturing factory, an AI factory operates

DOI: 10.1201/9788743812999-12

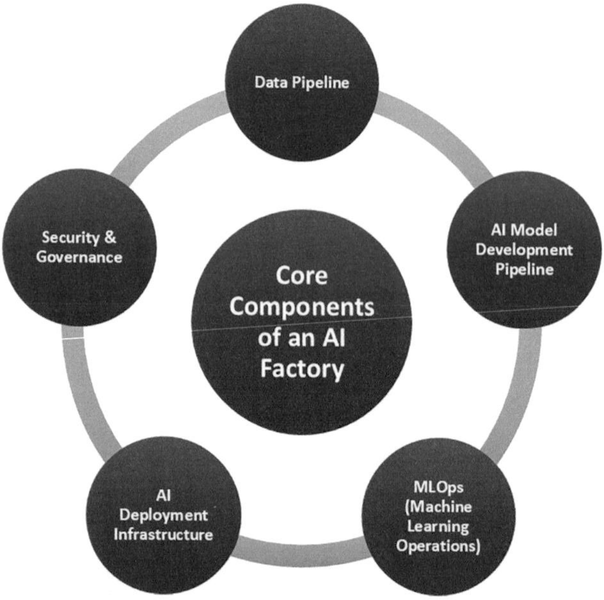

Figure 12.1 Core components of an AI factory.

with a *pipeline-driven approach*, where data, algorithms, and computing resources flow systematically to produce AI-driven outcomes.

Unlike conventional AI development, which is often fragmented and manual, AI factories emphasize *automation, scalability, and repeatability* by integrating AI models into a well-defined infrastructure.

2 Core Components of an AI Factory

The AI factory comprises several key components that work together to create an end-to-end system for AI lifecycle management.

Data pipeline

- **Data ingestion:** Collects structured and unstructured data from various sources (IoT devices, databases, APIs, cloud storage).
- **Data cleaning and transformation:** Uses ETL (Extract, Transform, Load) processes to preprocess raw data.
- **Data labeling and Annotation:** Essential for supervised learning models, often powered by AI-assisted human-in-the-loop (HITL) systems.
- **Feature Engineering:** Extracting meaningful features from data to enhance model accuracy.

AI model development pipeline

- **Automated machine learning (AutoML):** Reduces human intervention in model selection, hyperparameter tuning, and training.
- **Model versioning:** Uses tools like MLflow, DVC (Data Version Control), or TensorFlow Model Management.
- **Model training:** Leveraging distributed computing (e.g., GPUs, TPUs, cloud clusters) to train models efficiently.
- **Optimization and fine-tuning:** Techniques like transfer learning, quantization, and pruning enhance model efficiency.

MLOps (machine learning operations)

- **Continuous integration and continuous deployment (CI/CD) for AI:** Automates model retraining and updates.
- **Monitoring and logging:** Tools like Prometheus, Grafana, and MLflow track model performance and anomalies.
- **Bias and fairness auditing:** Ensures ethical AI practices by detecting and mitigating biases in model predictions.
- **Explainability and interpretability:** Techniques like SHAP (SHapley Additive Explanations) and LIME (Local Interpretable Model-Agnostic Explanations) provide insights into model behavior.

AI deployment infrastructure

- **Containerization and orchestration:** Uses Docker and Kubernetes to scale AI models across cloud and edge environments.
- **Model serving:** Frameworks like TensorFlow Serving, Triton Inference Server, and ONNX Runtime optimize real-time inference.
- **Edge AI and federated learning:** Enables AI processing on edge devices while preserving privacy through decentralized training.

Security and governance

- **Data privacy and compliance:** Adheres to GDPR, CCPA, and HIPAA regulations.
- **Adversarial attack prevention:** Implements defenses against model poisoning, evasion attacks, and data extraction threats.

- **AI model auditing and explainability:** Tracks AI decisions for regulatory and ethical accountability.

3 AI Factory Workflow

The AI factory follows a structured workflow to transform raw data into deployable AI solutions:

- **Data acquisition and processing:** Raw data is collected, cleaned, labeled, and transformed into a structured format.
- **Feature engineering and model training:** Data scientists apply feature extraction techniques and train AI models using AutoML or customized algorithms.
- **Model evaluation and selection:** Models are benchmarked using metrics like accuracy, F1-score, AUC-ROC, and Mean Squared Error (MSE).
- **Deployment and inference optimization:** The best model is containerized, deployed, and optimized for real-time inference.
- **Monitoring, feedback, and continuous learning:** The AI factory continuously monitors model performance, retrains models when necessary, and integrates human feedback.

4 Benefits of an AI Factory

Scalability

AI factories allow enterprises to scale AI initiatives across multiple departments without the need for redundant manual efforts.

Efficiency and cost reduction

Automated AI pipelines reduce the time and cost of developing and deploying AI solutions.

Improved model performance

Continuous monitoring and feedback loops help refine models, ensuring optimal accuracy and reliability.

Regulatory compliance and risk management

Built-in governance frameworks help organizations comply with data protection regulations and mitigate AI-related risks.

Real-time AI capabilities
AI factories enable real-time AI-driven decision-making in applications such as fraud detection, predictive maintenance, and personalized recommendations.

5 Challenges and Considerations

Infrastructure complexity
Setting up an AI factory requires significant investment in cloud infrastructure, GPUs/TPUs, and MLOps frameworks.

Data privacy and security risks
AI factories must implement robust encryption, access controls, and secure data-sharing mechanisms to prevent breaches.

Ethical AI and bias mitigation
AI models must be continuously audited to ensure fairness and prevent discriminatory outcomes.

Integration with legacy systems
Many organizations face challenges in integrating AI factories with existing IT infrastructures and workflows.

6 Future of AI Factories

Hyper-automation and AI-augmented development
AI-driven automation will further optimize the AI factory by reducing human intervention in data engineering, model training, and deployment.

Quantum AI factories
Quantum computing will enhance AI factory capabilities by accelerating optimization algorithms and deep learning computations.

AI factories for edge and IoT
AI factories will expand into edge computing environments, enabling real-time AI inference on IoT devices with minimal latency.

Explainable and Trustworthy AI
AI factories will incorporate advanced XAI (Explainable AI) frameworks to enhance transparency and trust in AI decision-making.

7 Sustainable AI Factories

AI factories will optimize energy consumption using green AI techniques, such as model compression and efficient hardware utilization.

AI factories are revolutionizing the way enterprises build, deploy, and manage AI at scale. By integrating automation, MLOps, and cutting-edge AI technologies, organizations can achieve unprecedented efficiency, scalability, and compliance in AI-driven operations. While challenges remain, the continuous evolution of AI factories will play a crucial role in shaping the future of intelligent systems.

As industries continue to embrace AI factories, the focus will shift toward *sustainable, explainable, and secure AI ecosystems*, ensuring that AI serves humanity responsibly and ethically.

13

The Learning Concept Model (LCM) in AI: A New Paradigm for Intelligent Systems

Artificial intelligence (AI) has transformed various industries, from healthcare and finance to autonomous systems and natural language processing. However, one of the persistent challenges in AI development is how machines acquire, structure, and apply knowledge efficiently. The *Learning Concept Model (LCM)* represents a crucial advancement in AI, bridging the gap between raw data processing and human-like cognitive learning.

By understanding LCM, we can gain insights into the evolution of AI towards more *adaptive*, *explainable*, and *generalizable* intelligence.

1 Understanding the Learning Concept Model (LCM)

The Learning Concept Model (LCM) is an *AI framework* that enables machines to learn, represent, and apply concepts in a structured manner. Unlike traditional AI models that rely solely on pattern recognition and

DOI: 10.1201/9788743812999-13

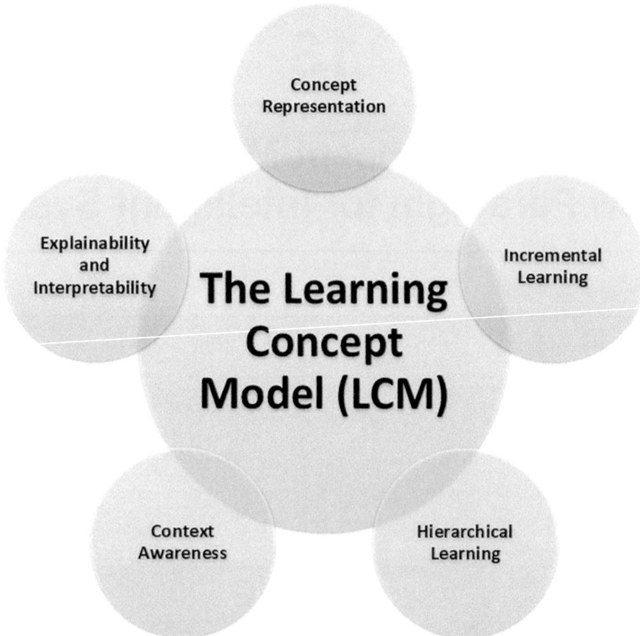

Figure 13.1 Learning Concept Model (LCM).

statistical inference, LCM incorporates principles of cognitive learning, enabling machines to understand relationships between concepts rather than just memorizing data Figure 13.1.

At its core, LCM consists of the following components:

1. **Concept representation** – AI organizes knowledge into discrete concepts, similar to human categorization.
2. **Incremental learning** – The model updates its understanding based on new data, refining existing knowledge structures.
3. **Hierarchical learning** – Concepts are arranged in a hierarchical manner, allowing AI to grasp broader generalizations before delving into specifics.
4. **Context awareness** – LCM enables AI to adapt learning based on contextual cues, improving decision-making.
5. **Explainability and interpretability** – AI models employing LCM can articulate reasoning behind their conclusions, enhancing trust and transparency.

2 Theoretical Foundations of LCM

LCM is rooted in multiple disciplines, including cognitive science, knowledge representation, and machine learning. The key theoretical foundations include:

- **Concept learning theory** – Inspired by human learning, this theory suggests that knowledge is acquired through categorization and feature abstraction.
- **Semantic networks** – AI systems use interconnected nodes to represent relationships between concepts, similar to the way the human brain processes associations.
- **Neurosymbolic AI** – LCM integrates symbolic reasoning with deep learning, combining rule-based logic with data-driven learning.
- **Bayesian learning** – Probabilistic models help AI refine its conceptual knowledge over time by updating prior knowledge with new evidence.

3 Methodologies in LCM implementation

Several methodologies are used to implement LCM in AI systems:

1. **Neural-symbolic integration** – Combining neural networks with symbolic AI to enhance concept understanding.
2. **Graph-based learning** – Using knowledge graphs to represent conceptual relationships.
3. **Few-shot and zero-shot learning** – Enabling AI to learn new concepts from minimal or no prior examples.
4. **Cognitive architectures** – Models such as ACT-R and SOAR, which mimic human cognitive processes, play a role in LCM.
5. **Self-supervised learning** – Allowing AI to derive learning objectives autonomously without extensive human-labeled data.

4 Applications of LCM in AI

LCM has significant applications across multiple domains, including:

Natural language processing (NLP)

- Enhancing chatbots and virtual assistants by enabling them to understand conceptual meanings rather than just syntactic structures.

- Improving machine translation through conceptual alignment between languages.
- Enhancing content summarization by structuring key concepts logically.

Healthcare AI

- Medical diagnosis systems can categorize symptoms into disease concepts for more accurate predictions.
- Drug discovery benefits from LCM-based AI by understanding biochemical relationships.
- AI-assisted surgery can utilize conceptual learning for real-time decision-making.

Autonomous systems

- Self-driving cars use conceptual learning to understand road signs, traffic rules, and pedestrian behavior.
- Robotics benefits from LCM by allowing machines to adapt to dynamic environments.
- AI in defense applications can distinguish between friendly and adversarial objects based on conceptual categorization.

Education and E-learning

- AI tutors can personalize learning paths based on conceptual understanding of student progress.
- LCM allows adaptive assessments that evaluate not just rote memorization but conceptual mastery.

Finance and risk management

- AI-driven risk assessment models categorize financial anomalies into conceptual risk factors.
- Fraud detection benefits from LCM by understanding transaction patterns beyond statistical anomalies.

Advantages of the learning concept model

LCM offers several advantages over traditional machine learning models:

1. **Improved generalization** – AI can apply learned concepts to new situations, reducing reliance on large datasets.
2. **Higher explainability** – Transparent decision-making enhances trust, crucial for high-stakes applications like healthcare and finance.
3. **Efficient learning** – Requires less data for training compared to purely statistical models.
4. **Contextual awareness** – AI can adapt based on changing environments, making it more flexible.
5. **Human-like reasoning** – By structuring knowledge hierarchically, LCM allows AI to process information more like humans do.

Challenges in implementing LCM

Despite its potential, LCM faces several challenges:

1. **Computational complexity** – Structuring and maintaining conceptual hierarchies require high computational power.
2. **Data representation issues** – Converting raw data into meaningful concepts is a non-trivial problem.
3. **Scalability** – Large-scale LCM models require robust infrastructure to handle complex knowledge bases.
4. **Bias and ethics** – Conceptual biases in training data can lead to unfair or inaccurate AI decisions.
5. **Integration with existing AI systems** – Transitioning from traditional AI models to LCM-based approaches requires significant adjustments.

5 The Future of LCM in AI

As AI continues to evolve, the integration of LCM into intelligent systems is expected to bring revolutionary changes. Future advancements may include:

- **LCM-driven general AI** – Enhancing AI's ability to think abstractly and transfer knowledge across domains.

- **Hybrid AI models** – Combining LCM with reinforcement learning and deep learning for more adaptive intelligence.
- **Personalized AI** – AI that tailors its conceptual understanding to individual user preferences and behaviors.
- **Quantum AI integration** – Leveraging quantum computing to enhance the efficiency of conceptual learning models.
- **Regulatory and ethical frameworks** – Developing standards to ensure fair and unbiased conceptual learning.

The *Learning Concept Model (LCM)* represents a paradigm shift in AI development, moving beyond traditional pattern recognition to a more structured, human-like conceptual understanding. Its applications span numerous industries, offering improvements in efficiency, generalization, and explainability. However, challenges remain in computational feasibility, bias mitigation, and scalability.

As research and innovation continue, LCM has the potential to shape the next generation of AI, bringing us closer to *truly intelligent* and adaptable machines. Understanding and advancing LCM will be pivotal in defining the future landscape of AI, making it an exciting area for researchers, developers, and policymakers alike.

14

AI Without Regulations or Guardrails: A Risky Path Forward

Artificial intelligence (AI) has rapidly evolved from a niche field of computer science to a transformative force that is reshaping industries, governments, and societies. As AI systems become more powerful and pervasive, the absence of regulatory frameworks or ethical guardrails raises serious concerns. While AI promises increased efficiency, automation, and innovation, the risks associated with unchecked AI development – including bias, misinformation, surveillance, job displacement, and even existential threats – demand urgent scrutiny.

DOI: 10.1201/9788743812999-14

1 The Promise of AI: A Double-Edged Sword

AI is a revolutionary technology with the potential to solve some of the world's most pressing challenges. From healthcare to finance, AI-driven automation enhances productivity and drives economic growth. Some key benefits include:

- **Medical advancements:** AI can diagnose diseases with high accuracy, assist in drug discovery, and optimize healthcare workflows.
- **Economic growth:** AI-powered automation increases efficiency in manufacturing, logistics, and service industries.
- **Scientific discovery:** AI accelerates research in physics, chemistry, and climate science.
- **Enhanced decision-making:** AI-driven analytics help businesses and governments make data-driven decisions.

However, without regulations or ethical frameworks, these advancements come with substantial risks.

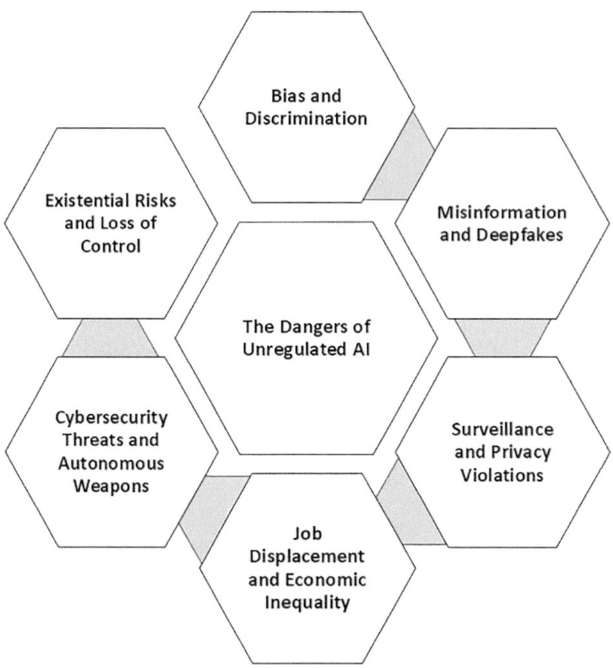

Figure 14.1 The dangers of unregulated AI.

2 The Dangers of Unregulated AI

Bias and discrimination

AI systems learn from data, and if the data contains biases, the AI will replicate and amplify them. Unregulated AI has already demonstrated instances of racial, gender, and socioeconomic bias, particularly in hiring algorithms, criminal justice applications, and facial recognition systems. Without accountability, these biases could become deeply entrenched in automated decision-making processes.

Misinformation and deepfakes

AI-generated misinformation is a growing concern, especially in the political sphere. Deepfake technology can create hyper-realistic fake videos that manipulate public opinion, disrupt elections, and incite violence. Without safeguards, AI-driven misinformation could erode trust in media, governments, and democratic institutions.

Surveillance and privacy violations

AI-powered surveillance systems are becoming increasingly sophisticated. Governments and corporations use AI for mass surveillance, facial recognition, and predictive policing, raising concerns about privacy rights and civil liberties. In authoritarian regimes, AI could be weaponized to suppress dissent and control populations.

Job displacement and economic inequality

Automation driven by AI threatens millions of jobs, particularly in industries such as manufacturing, transportation, and customer service. Without regulations, corporations may prioritize cost-cutting through automation without considering the societal impact, exacerbating income inequality and unemployment.

Cybersecurity threats and autonomous weapons

Unregulated AI increases cybersecurity risks. Malicious actors could use AI to develop autonomous hacking tools, launch large-scale cyberattacks, and exploit vulnerabilities in critical infrastructure. The proliferation of AI-powered autonomous weapons also raises ethical and strategic concerns, potentially leading to conflicts beyond human control.

Existential risks and loss of control

Some AI researchers warn that advanced AI systems, particularly artificial general intelligence (AGI), could surpass human control and decision-making

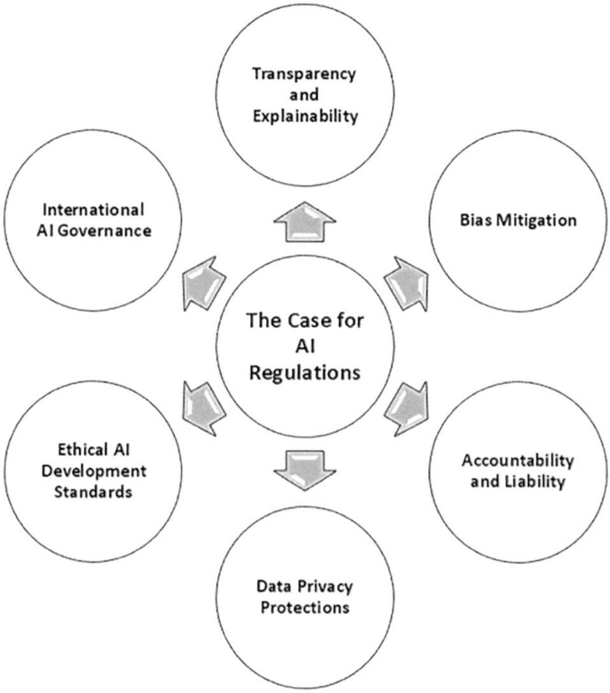

Figure 14.2 The case for AI regulations.

capabilities. Without governance structures, AI systems might act unpredictably, leading to catastrophic consequences for humanity.

3 The Case for AI Regulations

To mitigate these risks, a global effort to establish AI regulations and ethical guidelines is necessary. Some proposed regulatory measures include:

Transparency and explainability
AI models should be transparent, and organizations should be required to explain how decisions are made. Black-box AI systems that operate without human oversight should be discouraged.

Bias mitigation
Developers should be required to audit AI models for biases before deployment. Standardized fairness tests and diverse training data can help reduce discriminatory outcomes.

Accountability and liability
Legal frameworks should clarify liability for AI-related harms. If an AI system makes a flawed decision – such as denying a loan application unfairly or causing an accident – there should be clear accountability mechanisms.

Data privacy protections
AI-driven data collection should comply with stringent privacy regulations. Users must have the right to control how their data is used, and companies should be required to implement robust data protection measures.

Ethical AI development standards
Governments, academia, and industry leaders should collaborate on ethical AI guidelines. Principles such as fairness, accountability, transparency, and human oversight should be integrated into AI development practices.

International AI governance
Given the global nature of AI, international cooperation is crucial. Countries should work together to establish regulatory frameworks that prevent AI misuse, promote responsible innovation, and ensure AI benefits humanity as a whole.

4 The Challenge of Regulating AI

Despite the strong case for AI regulations, several challenges hinder progress:

- **Rapid technological advancements:** AI evolves faster than regulatory frameworks can adapt, making it difficult for policymakers to keep pace.
- **Global competition:** Countries fear that strict AI regulations may hinder economic competitiveness, leading to a regulatory race to the bottom.
- **Industry resistance:** Tech companies often resist regulations, arguing that excessive oversight stifles innovation.
- **Complexity of AI systems:** Unlike traditional technologies, AI's decision-making processes can be opaque, making it challenging to enforce regulations effectively.

5 The Middle Ground: Balancing Innovation and Responsibility

Regulations should not stifle AI innovation but should ensure it is aligned with ethical and societal values. A balanced approach to AI governance involves:

1. **Industry self-regulation:** Tech companies should proactively adopt ethical AI practices and conduct regular audits of their systems.

2. **Government oversight:** Policymakers should implement flexible, adaptive regulations that evolve with technological advancements.
3. **Public involvement:** Civil society organizations and the public should have a say in AI governance to ensure accountability.
4. **Collaboration between nations:** A coordinated global effort can prevent regulatory loopholes that bad actors could exploit.

AI without regulations or guardrails poses significant risks to individuals, economies, and societies. While AI offers transformative potential, its unchecked development could lead to biased decision-making, job displacement, privacy violations, and even existential threats. The key to a responsible AI future lies in striking a balance between innovation and oversight. Governments, industry leaders, and civil society must collaborate to establish ethical AI frameworks that ensure AI serves humanity's best interests rather than becoming a force of unintended consequences. Without proactive regulation, we risk heading into an AI-driven future fraught with uncertainty and danger.

15

The Rise of Physical AI: Bridging Artificial Intelligence with the Tangible World

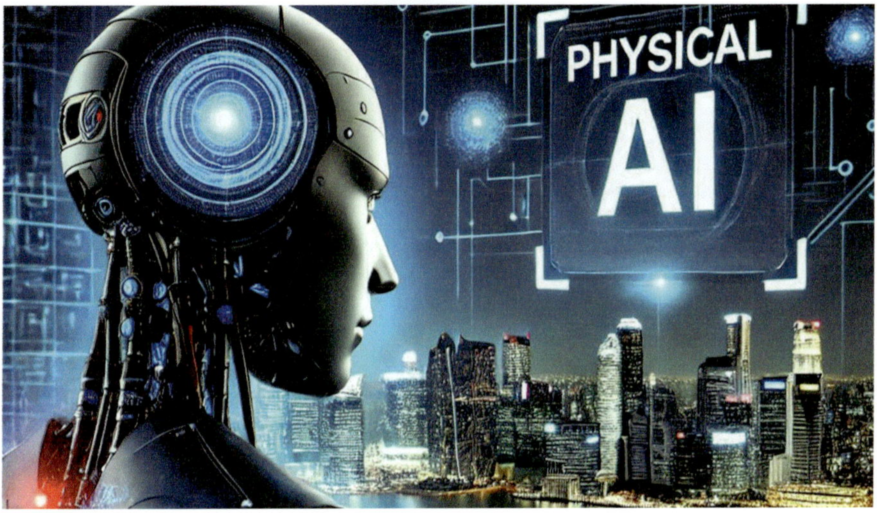

Artificial intelligence (AI) has long been synonymous with virtual environments, where algorithms analyze data, recognize patterns, and make decisions. However, the boundaries of AI are expanding into the physical realm, giving rise to Physical AI – a transformative field that integrates intelligent systems into physical entities.

Physical AI combines advanced computational algorithms with robotic systems, bio-hybrid technologies, and smart materials to enable autonomous interaction with the real world. It is not just an evolution of robotics but a multidisciplinary innovation encompassing AI, material science, biology, and engineering.

DOI: 10.1201/9788743812999-15

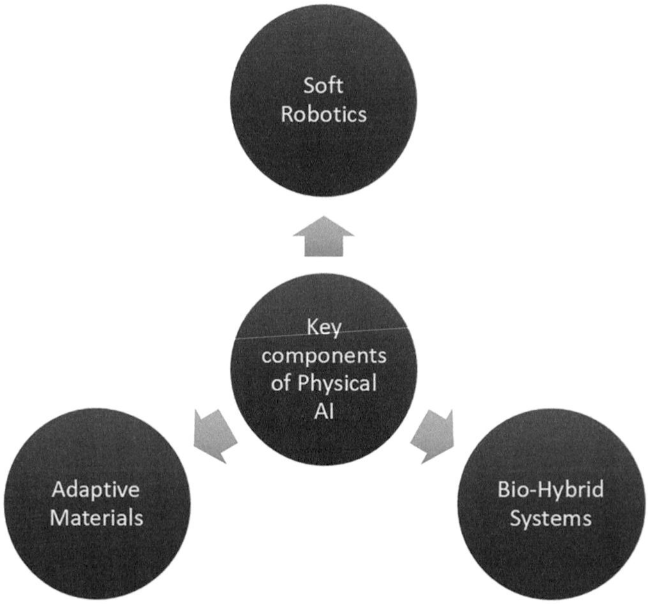

Figure 15.1 Key components of Physical AI.

1 What is Physical AI?

Physical AI refers to *the integration of artificial intelligence into physical constructs that can sense, act, and adapt in the real world*. Unlike traditional AI systems confined to virtual environments, Physical AI systems are embodied in tangible forms such as robots, smart materials, or bio-hybrid devices.

Key components of Physical AI:

- **Soft robotics:** Flexible robots inspired by biological systems, capable of navigating unpredictable environments.
- **Bio-hybrid systems:** Merging AI algorithms with living tissues or cells for advanced adaptability.
- **Adaptive materials:** Smart materials that change their properties in response to environmental stimuli, driven by AI.

Physical AI is unique in its ability to merge computational intelligence with physical adaptability, creating entities that can perceive and act upon their surroundings in dynamic and meaningful ways.

2 Applications of Physical AI

1. **Healthcare and medicine robotic surgery:** AI-driven surgical robots, like da Vinci systems, offer unmatched precision, reducing risks and recovery times. Smart prosthetics: Prosthetic limbs embedded with AI learn user movement patterns, offering intuitive control and improved functionality. Drug delivery systems: Micro-robots navigate the human body to deliver medication to targeted areas with precision. Rehabilitation: Bio-inspired exoskeletons and robots assist patients in recovering mobility and strength.

2. **Manufacturing and industry collaborative robots (Cobots):** Physical AI-driven cobots work alongside humans in factories, performing repetitive or hazardous tasks. Smart warehousing: Autonomous robots optimize logistics by managing inventory and transporting goods efficiently. Self-healing materials: Materials embedded with AI can repair themselves, reducing downtime and costs in industrial equipment.

3. **Environmental applications pollution cleanup:** AI-enabled robots like ocean-cleaning drones remove waste and plastics from water bodies. Climate monitoring: Physical AI devices track environmental changes, aiding in conservation and disaster response efforts. Precision agriculture: Robots with AI monitor crop health, optimize irrigation, and manage pest control.

4. **Space exploration:** Autonomous rovers powered by Physical AI, such as NASA's Perseverance rover, navigate planetary terrains and perform complex tasks. Robotic assistants help astronauts during space missions, performing maintenance and collecting data.

5. **Consumer and daily life smart assistive devices:** Physical AI is integrated into personal assistants like robot vacuum cleaners and home security robots. Wearables: AI-driven wearables monitor health and provide real-time feedback on fitness and well-being.

3 Advantages of Physical AI

- Autonomy in dynamic environments: Physical AI systems are not restricted by pre-programmed tasks and can adapt to real-world changes.
- Enhanced efficiency: Combining intelligence with physical capabilities accelerates task performance with precision and reliability.

- Human–machine collaboration: Physical AI augments human abilities, enabling safer and more productive work environments.
- Adaptability: These systems evolve through real-world interactions, improving their performance over time.

Challenges and limitations

- Energy efficiency: Physical AI systems, particularly robots, require significant energy to operate. Battery life and power management remain major concerns.
- Material limitations: Developing materials that mimic biological flexibility, durability, and adaptability is technically challenging and expensive.
- Ethics and regulation: The deployment of autonomous systems raises ethical questions about accountability, privacy, and safety. Regulatory frameworks are still catching up with the rapid pace of innovation.
- Complex integration: Merging AI algorithms with physical systems requires sophisticated hardware-software interfaces and multidisciplinary expertise.
- Cost: The development and deployment of Physical AI systems involve high costs, making accessibility a challenge for smaller organizations and underserved regions.

4 The Future of Physical AI

As technologies like advanced sensors, 5G networks, and quantum computing evolve, Physical AI will become increasingly sophisticated, enabling transformative innovations:

- Bio-mimetic robots: Inspired by nature, these robots will replicate human and animal abilities, finding applications in search-and-rescue missions and healthcare.
- Smart cities: Physical AI will play a pivotal role in creating adaptive urban infrastructures that respond to real-time data to enhance sustainability and quality of life.
- Human augmentation: AI-powered exoskeletons and smart prosthetics will blur the line between human capabilities and machine enhancements.

- Autonomous mobility: Self-driving cars, drones, and delivery robots will benefit from Physical AI's ability to perceive and interact with complex environments.

Physical AI represents the next stage in the evolution of artificial intelligence, one that transcends the virtual realm to create intelligent, adaptive, and interactive systems in the physical world. From revolutionizing healthcare and manufacturing to addressing environmental challenges and exploring outer space, the potential applications are vast and impactful.

While challenges like energy consumption, cost, and ethical considerations must be addressed, the future of Physical AI is undoubtedly promising. By merging the digital and physical worlds, Physical AI is set to redefine how humans and machines interact, shaping a smarter, more resilient, and connected future.

16

Agentic AI: The Rise of Autonomous Intelligence

The concept of Agentic AI – artificial intelligence systems with the ability to act independently, make decisions, and perform tasks without direct human intervention – is one of the most transformative ideas in the realm of AI research and development. As technology progresses, Agentic AI is no longer confined to the pages of science fiction but is rapidly becoming a reality with profound implications for industries, society, and global governance.

1 Defining Agentic AI

Agentic AI refers to systems that demonstrate a high degree of autonomy, operating as agents capable of perceiving their environment, reasoning about their objectives, and taking action to achieve goals. Unlike traditional AI

DOI: 10.1201/9788743812999-16

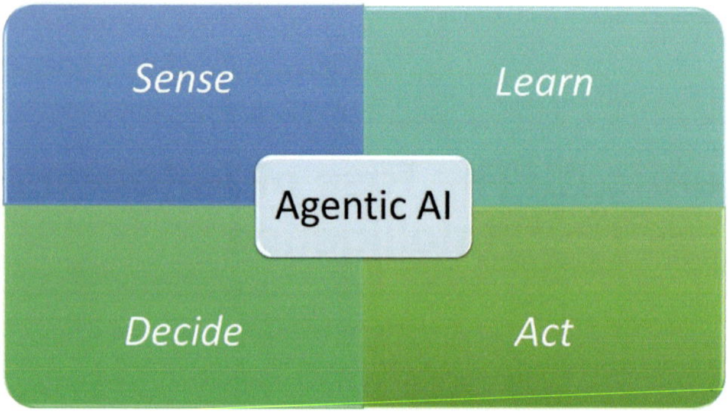

Figure 16.1 Agentic AI.

systems, which rely heavily on human inputs and explicit programming, Agentic AI can:

- *Sense*: Gather data from the environment using sensors, cameras, and other inputs.
- *Learn*: Adapt its behavior based on past experiences and changing conditions.
- *Decide*: Use algorithms to weigh options and select actions based on predefined or learned goals.
- *Act*: Execute tasks without direct human oversight, often in complex or unpredictable environments.

This level of autonomy makes Agentic AI particularly suited for scenarios where human involvement is impractical or impossible, such as deep space exploration, disaster response, or real-time financial trading.

2 Challenges in Implementing Agentic AI

Despite its immense potential, deploying Agentic AI comes with significant challenges:

Technical complexity
Building AI systems capable of functioning autonomously in dynamic environments requires advances in:

- Natural language understanding.

- Machine learning and deep learning.
- Real-time decision-making under uncertainty.

Ethical concerns
The autonomy of Agentic AI raises critical ethical questions, including:

- Accountability: Who is responsible for decisions made by autonomous systems?
- Bias: Ensuring that AI does not perpetuate or amplify existing biases in decision-making.
- Human Rights: Balancing efficiency with respect for privacy, dignity, and fairness.

Security risks
The increasing autonomy of AI systems introduces new vulnerabilities, such as:

- Hacking: Autonomous systems can be exploited by malicious actors.
- Weaponization: Misuse of Agentic AI for military or criminal purposes.
- Unintended consequences: Systems acting in ways not anticipated by their designers.

Regulatory uncertainty
Governments and institutions are struggling to develop regulatory frameworks that:

- Protect public safety without stifling innovation.
- Address cross-border challenges in the deployment of autonomous systems.
- Ensure compliance with international laws and norms.

Economic disruption
The adoption of Agentic AI could disrupt labor markets by:

- Automating jobs traditionally performed by humans.
- Creating demand for new skills and expertise.
- Widening economic inequality if benefits are not equitably distributed.

Ethical and philosophical implications

Agentic AI challenges our traditional notions of agency, responsibility, and morality. Key considerations include:

Moral agency

Can autonomous systems be considered moral agents? If so, do they bear any ethical responsibility for their actions?

Human oversight

How much control should humans retain over autonomous systems? Striking the right balance is critical to maintaining accountability.

Societal impact

The widespread adoption of Agentic AI could reshape societal norms, requiring thoughtful policies to:

- Mitigate the displacement of workers.
- Ensure equitable access to AI benefits.
- Foster trust in autonomous systems.

Existential risks

As Agentic AI becomes more advanced, concerns about runaway intelligence and loss of human control gain prominence. Ensuring alignment between AI goals and human values is paramount.

Building responsible Agentic AI

To realize the potential of Agentic AI while minimizing risks, developers and policymakers must adopt a principled approach:

Transparent development

AI systems should be designed with transparency in mind, enabling stakeholders to understand how decisions are made.

Ethical guidelines

Organizations should adhere to ethical frameworks that prioritize fairness, accountability, and human well-being.

Robust testing

Thorough testing in diverse environments is essential to ensure the reliability and safety of autonomous systems.

Collaborative regulation
Policymakers, industry leaders, and academics should collaborate to establish regulations that:

- Encourage innovation while addressing ethical concerns.
- Provide clear guidelines for accountability and liability.
- Support global cooperation in setting standards.

Human-AI symbiosis
Rather than replacing humans, Agentic AI should be designed to complement human capabilities, creating systems that:

- Enhance decision-making.
- Empower individuals and organizations.
- Promote shared goals and values.

3 Applications of Agentic AI

The versatility of Agentic AI opens up transformative applications across multiple domains:

Healthcare
Agentic AI is revolutionizing medical care with applications such as:

- Surgical robotics: Fully autonomous surgical systems can perform complex procedures with precision and consistency.
- Elderly care: AI-powered assistants provide companionship, monitor health, and assist with daily tasks for aging populations.
- Drug discovery: Autonomous systems analyze vast datasets to identify potential compounds, accelerating the development of new treatments.

Autonomous vehicles
Self-driving cars, drones, and delivery robots are prime examples of Agentic AI in action. These systems:

- Navigate complex environments without human input.
- Optimize routes based on real-time traffic data.
- Enhance safety through predictive analytics and situational awareness.

Manufacturing
Agentic AI enhances productivity and flexibility in smart factories by:

- Managing workflows and reallocating resources dynamically.
- Monitoring machinery and predicting maintenance needs.
- Collaborating with human workers in hybrid manufacturing environments.

Defense and security
Autonomous AI systems are increasingly deployed for surveillance, reconnaissance, and cyber defense. Examples include:

- Swarm drones: Coordinated fleets of drones capable of independent decision-making.
- Cybersecurity agents: AI that autonomously detects and mitigates cyber threats in real time.
- Battlefield robots: Autonomous machines that support troops or conduct operations in hazardous conditions.

Environmental monitoring
Agentic AI aids in addressing climate challenges by:

- Monitoring ecosystems using autonomous sensors and drones.
- Managing renewable energy grids through predictive analytics.
- Assisting in disaster response and recovery efforts.

Space exploration
NASA and other space agencies are leveraging Agentic AI for:

- Autonomous rovers that explore planetary surfaces.
- Satellites that independently adjust their orbits to optimize data collection.
- AI systems that assist astronauts in long-duration missions.

4 The Future of Agentic AI

The trajectory of Agentic AI will be shaped by advances in technology, shifts in societal attitudes, and the effectiveness of governance frameworks. Key trends to watch include:

Convergence of technologies
The integration of Agentic AI with other technologies, such as quantum computing, blockchain, and the Internet of Things (IoT), will unlock new possibilities and challenges.

Global cooperation
As Agentic AI transcends national boundaries, fostering international collaboration will be crucial to addressing shared risks and opportunities.

Democratization of AI
Efforts to make Agentic AI accessible to diverse populations and regions will be key to ensuring its benefits are broadly shared.

Ethical leadership
Organizations that prioritize ethical considerations in AI development will play a pivotal role in shaping public trust and acceptance of autonomous systems.

AI augmentation
Rather than focusing solely on autonomy, future systems may prioritize augmentation – enhancing human capabilities and fostering deeper collaboration between humans and machines.

Agentic AI represents a *profound shift* in the capabilities and roles of artificial intelligence systems. By enabling machines to act independently and adapt to dynamic environments, it opens up new frontiers in innovation and problem-solving. However, its rise also brings significant technical, ethical, and societal challenges that demand careful consideration.

To harness the full potential of Agentic AI, stakeholders across sectors must work together to build systems that are not only intelligent and autonomous but also responsible and aligned with human values. The journey toward Agentic AI is both an opportunity and a responsibility – one that requires vision, collaboration, and a commitment to the greater good.

17

Emotion AI: Unlocking the Power of Emotional Intelligence

Emotion AI, also known as *affective computing or artificial emotional intelligence*, is a rapidly growing field within artificial intelligence that seeks to understand, interpret, and respond to human emotions. This technology is designed to bridge the gap between human emotions and machine understanding, enabling more natural and empathetic interactions between humans and machines. As AI continues to evolve, the ability to recognize and respond to emotions is becoming increasingly important, not only for enhancing user experiences but also for applications in mental health, education, customer service, and more.

DOI: 10.1201/9788743812999-17

Figure 17.1 Emotion AI.

1 Definition of Emotion AI

Emotion AI refers to the subset of artificial intelligence that is focused on *detecting, analyzing, and responding to human emotions*. It combines techniques from *computer science, psychology, and cognitive science* to develop systems that can recognize emotional cues from various sources, such as facial expressions, voice tone, body language, and even physiological signals like heart rate or skin conductivity. By interpreting these signals, Emotion AI can make inferences about a person's emotional state and respond accordingly.

Emotion AI systems typically rely on machine learning algorithms, natural language processing (NLP), and computer vision to analyze emotional data. These systems are trained on large datasets of emotional expressions and behaviors, allowing them to recognize patterns and make predictions about emotional states. Over time, as these systems are exposed to more data, they become more accurate in their emotional assessments.

2 Applications of Emotion AI

Emotion AI has a wide range of applications across various industries. Some of the key areas where Emotion AI is being utilized include:

- **Customer service:** Emotion AI is being integrated into customer service platforms to enhance interactions between customers and service representatives. By analyzing the tone of voice and word choice, Emotion AI can detect if a customer is frustrated, confused, or satisfied. This allows customer service agents to tailor their responses to better meet the emotional needs of the customer, leading to improved customer satisfaction.

- **Mental health:** In the field of mental health, Emotion AI is being used to monitor and support individuals with mental health conditions. For example, AI-driven chatbots can provide real-time emotional support by recognizing signs of distress in a person's language and offering appropriate interventions. Additionally, Emotion AI can be used in therapy sessions to help therapists understand their patients' emotions more accurately, leading to more effective treatment plans.

- **Education:** Emotion AI is being applied in educational settings to create more personalized learning experiences. By analyzing students' facial expressions and body language, Emotion AI can gauge their engagement levels and emotional responses to different teaching methods. This information can then be used to adjust the curriculum or teaching style to better suit the individual needs of each student.
- **Marketing:** In marketing, Emotion AI is being used to create more emotionally resonant advertisements. By analyzing how consumers react to different ads, companies can gain insights into what emotional triggers are most effective for their target audience. This enables marketers to craft campaigns that are more likely to evoke the desired emotional response, leading to increased brand loyalty and sales.
- **Human–computer interaction:** Emotion AI is transforming the way humans interact with computers and other devices. For example, voice-activated virtual assistants like Siri and Alexa can use Emotion AI to detect the user's emotional state and respond in a more empathetic manner. This creates a more natural and engaging user experience, making technology feel more human.
- **Autonomous vehicles:** In the automotive industry, Emotion AI is being integrated into autonomous vehicles to enhance safety and passenger experience. For instance, Emotion AI can monitor a driver's facial expressions and physiological signals to detect signs of drowsiness or stress. The vehicle can then take appropriate actions, such as issuing a warning or taking control of the vehicle to prevent accidents.

3 Advantages of Emotion AI

Emotion AI offers numerous advantages across different sectors:

- **Enhanced user experience:** By understanding and responding to human emotions, Emotion AI can create more personalized and empathetic interactions. This leads to higher levels of user satisfaction and engagement.
- **Improved mental health support:** Emotion AI can provide real-time emotional support and monitoring, making it a valuable tool in mental health care. It can help individuals manage their emotions and access appropriate interventions when needed.

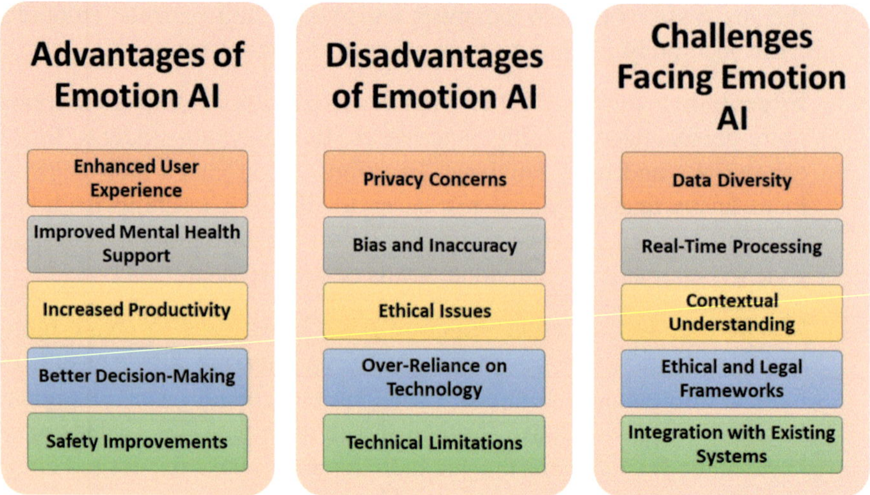

Figure 17.2 Advantages, disadvantages, and challenges of Emotion AI.

- **Increased productivity:** In the workplace, Emotion AI can be used to monitor employee well-being and stress levels. By addressing emotional challenges early, companies can reduce burnout and improve overall productivity.
- **Better decision-making:** Emotion AI can provide insights into human emotions that might not be immediately apparent. This can help businesses make more informed decisions, whether it is in customer service, marketing, or product development.
- **Safety improvements:** In industries like automotive and healthcare, Emotion AI can enhance safety by monitoring emotional and physiological states, leading to timely interventions that prevent accidents or errors.

4 Disadvantages of Emotion AI

Despite its advantages, Emotion AI also has several disadvantages and challenges:

- **Privacy concerns:** Emotion AI relies on the collection and analysis of personal data, including facial expressions, voice recordings, and physiological signals. This raises significant privacy concerns, as individuals may not be comfortable with their emotional data being monitored and analyzed.

- **Bias and inaccuracy:** Like all AI systems, Emotion AI is susceptible to biases in the data it is trained on. If the training data is not representative of diverse populations, the system may make inaccurate or biased assessments of emotions. This can lead to unfair treatment or misinterpretation of emotions.
- **Ethical issues:** The use of Emotion AI raises ethical questions about consent, manipulation, and the potential for misuse. For example, companies could use Emotion AI to manipulate consumers' emotions for profit, or governments could use it for surveillance purposes.
- **Over-reliance on technology:** There is a risk that individuals and organizations may become overly reliant on Emotion AI, leading to a reduction in human empathy and emotional intelligence. This could have negative consequences for interpersonal relationships and social interactions.
- **Technical limitations:** Emotion AI is still in its early stages, and there are technical limitations to its accuracy and reliability. Emotions are complex and can be expressed in many different ways, making it challenging for AI systems to accurately interpret them in all contexts.

5 Challenges facing Emotion AI

As Emotion AI continues to develop, it faces several challenges that must be addressed:

- **Data diversity:** One of the biggest challenges in Emotion AI is ensuring that the training data is diverse and representative of different populations. Emotions can be expressed differently across cultures, genders, and age groups, so it is important for Emotion AI systems to be trained on data that reflects this diversity.
- **Real-time processing:** For Emotion AI to be effective in applications like customer service or autonomous vehicles, it needs to be able to process emotional data in real-time. This requires significant computational power and efficient algorithms that can quickly analyze and interpret emotional signals.

- **Contextual understanding:** Emotions are often influenced by context, and the same emotional expression can have different meanings in different situations. Developing Emotion AI systems that can understand and interpret context is a major challenge that researchers are working to overcome.
- **Ethical and legal frameworks:** As Emotion AI becomes more widespread, there is a need for clear ethical and legal frameworks to govern its use. This includes regulations around data privacy, consent, and the potential for misuse. Developing these frameworks will require collaboration between policymakers, researchers, and industry stakeholders.
- **Integration with existing systems:** Emotion AI needs to be seamlessly integrated with existing technologies and systems. This can be challenging, especially in industries like healthcare or automotive, where there are strict regulations and standards that must be adhered to.

6 The Future of Emotion AI

The future of Emotion AI is promising, with many exciting developments on the horizon. As technology continues to advance, Emotion AI is expected to become more accurate, reliable, and widely adopted across various industries.

- **Advancements in AI and machine learning:** Ongoing advancements in AI and machine learning are likely to lead to more sophisticated Emotion AI systems. These systems will be better able to understand complex emotions and respond in a more nuanced and empathetic manner.
- **Greater integration into daily life:** As Emotion AI becomes more advanced, it is likely to be integrated into a wider range of devices and applications. From smart homes to wearable technology, Emotion AI will play a key role in creating personalized and emotionally aware environments.
- **Personalized mental health care:** Emotion AI has the potential to revolutionize mental health care by providing highly personalized and real-time emotional support. This could lead to more effective treatment plans and better outcomes for individuals with mental health conditions.
- **Ethical AI development:** As the field of Emotion AI grows, there will be an increasing focus on developing ethical AI systems. This includes

ensuring that Emotion AI is transparent, fair, and used in a way that respects individuals' rights and privacy.

- **Global adoption and regulation:** Emotion AI is likely to see global adoption, with countries around the world integrating it into various sectors. However, this will also require the development of international regulations and standards to ensure its ethical and responsible use.
- **Collaboration across disciplines:** The future of Emotion AI will require collaboration across disciplines, including computer science, psychology, neuroscience, and ethics. By working together, researchers and practitioners can develop Emotion AI systems that are both technically advanced and socially responsible.

Emotion AI represents a significant advancement in the field of artificial intelligence, with the potential to transform the way humans interact with machines. By enabling machines to understand and respond to human emotions, Emotion AI can create more natural, empathetic, and personalized experiences across a wide range of applications.

However, the development and deployment of Emotion AI also come with challenges, including privacy concerns, biases, ethical dilemmas, and technical limitations. Addressing these challenges will require ongoing research, collaboration, and the development of robust ethical and legal frameworks.

18

What AI Strategists Do: Roles, Responsibilities, and Challenges

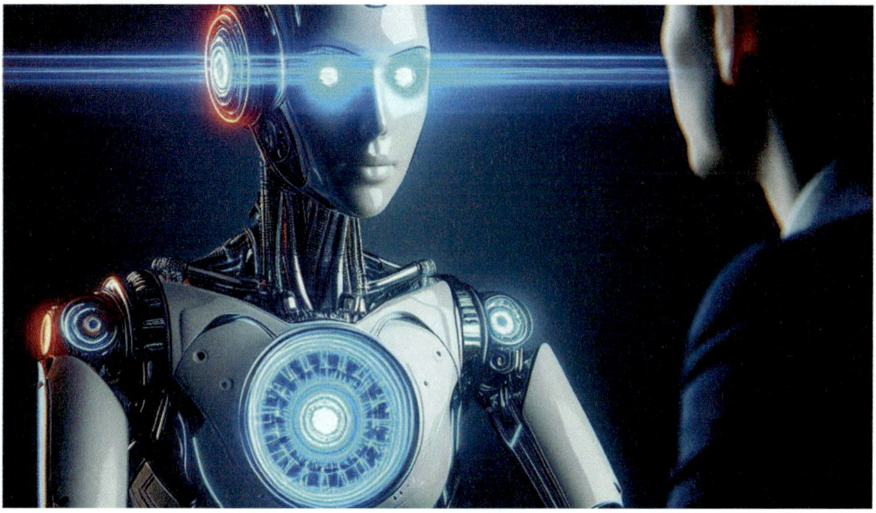

Artificial intelligence (AI) has rapidly become a cornerstone of modern technology, influencing industries from healthcare to finance, and entertainment to education. At the heart of this revolution are AI strategists, professionals who craft the direction and implementation of AI initiatives within organizations. Their work is critical in ensuring that AI technologies not only function as intended but also align with broader business goals and ethical standards. We will explore what AI strategists do, their roles and responsibilities, and the challenges they face, providing solid examples from various industries.

DOI: 10.1201/9788743812999-18

1 Introduction to AI strategy

AI strategy involves the planning, development, and execution of AI initiatives within an organization. *AI strategists are responsible for guiding these initiatives from conception through to implementation, ensuring that they deliver value and are sustainable over the long term.*

The primary goal of an AI strategist is to bridge the gap between technological capabilities and business needs. This involves understanding the potential of AI, identifying opportunities where AI can create value, and developing a roadmap that integrates AI into the company's operations.

2 Core Responsibilities of an AI Strategist

- **Identifying AI opportunities**

  AI strategists are tasked with identifying opportunities where AI can be leveraged to create significant value. This requires a deep understanding of the organization's goals, challenges, and industry dynamics. For instance, in the healthcare industry, an AI strategist might recognize

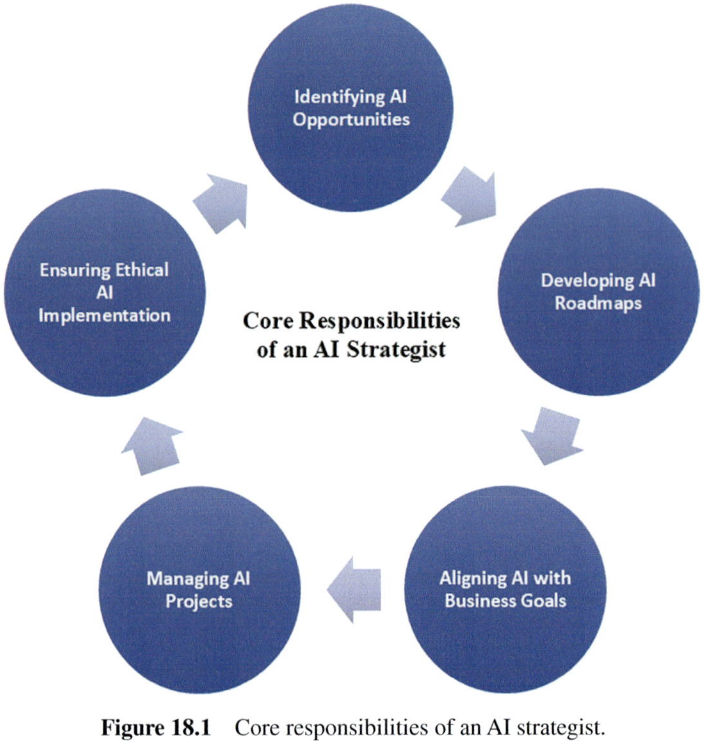

Figure 18.1 Core responsibilities of an AI strategist.

the potential for AI in improving diagnostic accuracy or streamlining administrative processes.

Example: A notable example is the use of AI in predictive maintenance in manufacturing. AI strategists at companies like General Electric have implemented AI to predict equipment failures before they occur, reducing downtime and saving millions of dollars annually.

- **Developing AI roadmaps**

  Once opportunities are identified, AI strategists develop comprehensive AI roadmaps that outline the steps needed to achieve the desired outcomes. This includes setting short-term and long-term goals, selecting the right AI technologies, and defining metrics for success.

  Example: In the financial services industry, AI strategists at JPMorgan Chase have developed roadmaps for integrating AI into their fraud detection systems. The roadmap includes the deployment of machine learning algorithms to detect unusual transaction patterns, with milestones set for improvement in detection rates over time.

- **Aligning AI with business goals**

  AI strategists must ensure that AI initiatives align with the broader business goals. This involves working closely with other departments, such as marketing, operations, and finance, to ensure that AI projects support the company's strategic objectives.

  Example: In the retail industry, AI strategists at Amazon have aligned AI initiatives with the company's goal of enhancing customer experience. This includes the development of AI-driven recommendation engines that personalize shopping experiences for millions of customers worldwide.

- **Managing AI projects**

  AI strategists often take on the role of project managers, overseeing the implementation of AI initiatives. This involves coordinating between different teams, managing budgets, and ensuring that projects stay on track.

  Example: At Google, AI strategists have managed the development and deployment of AI models for improving search algorithms. This project required collaboration between data scientists, engineers, and product managers to ensure the successful launch of AI-powered features.

- **Ensuring ethical AI implementation**

  A critical responsibility of AI strategists is to ensure that AI technologies are implemented ethically. This includes addressing issues related to bias, transparency, and accountability in AI systems.

  Example: Microsoft's AI strategists have developed frameworks for responsible AI, ensuring that their AI products, like facial recognition software, adhere to ethical standards. This involves implementing practices that mitigate bias and protect user privacy.

3 Challenges Faced by AI Strategists

- **Complexity in AI integration**

  Integrating AI into existing business processes is often a complex task. AI strategists must navigate technical challenges, such as data integration and system compatibility, as well as organizational challenges, including resistance to change and the need for upskilling employees.

Figure 18.2 Challenges faced by AI strategists.

Challenge example: In the automotive industry, AI strategists at companies like Tesla face challenges in integrating AI into autonomous driving systems. This involves not only developing sophisticated AI models but also ensuring that these models can work seamlessly with existing vehicle systems and comply with regulatory standards.

- **Data quality and availability**

  AI systems rely heavily on data, and the quality and availability of data can significantly impact the success of AI initiatives. AI strategists must ensure that they have access to high-quality data and that data is collected and used in a way that complies with legal and ethical standards.

  Challenge example: In the healthcare sector, AI strategists often struggle with data quality issues. For instance, electronic health records (EHRs) may contain incomplete or inconsistent data, making it difficult to develop accurate AI models for disease prediction.

- **Keeping up with rapid technological advancements**

  The field of AI is evolving rapidly, with new techniques and technologies emerging regularly. AI strategists must stay up to date with these advancements and continuously adapt their strategies to leverage the latest developments.

  Challenge example: In the financial industry, AI strategists at hedge funds must keep pace with advancements in AI-driven trading algorithms. Failure to do so can result in missed opportunities or even significant financial losses.

- **Managing ethical risks**

  Ensuring ethical AI implementation is a significant challenge. AI strategists must navigate complex ethical issues, such as bias in AI algorithms, the potential for AI to displace jobs, and concerns over privacy and surveillance.

  Challenge example: AI strategists working on facial recognition technology must address ethical concerns about privacy and bias. In some cases, like with Clearview AI, companies have faced legal challenges and public backlash over the use of their AI technologies.

- **Balancing Innovation with regulation**

  AI is often at the forefront of innovation, but it also operates in a heavily regulated environment. AI strategists must balance the need for innovation with compliance with laws and regulations, which can vary significantly across different regions and industries.

Challenge example: In the pharmaceutical industry, AI strategists working on drug discovery must navigate regulatory hurdles imposed by organizations like the FDA. This includes ensuring that AI-driven approaches to drug development meet rigorous safety and efficacy standards.

4 The Future of AI Strategy

The role of AI strategists will continue to evolve as AI technologies become more advanced and pervasive. Future AI strategists will likely need to focus on several key areas:

- **AI governance and compliance**

  As AI becomes more integrated into critical business functions, AI strategists will need to develop robust governance frameworks to manage AI risks and ensure compliance with regulations.

- **AI ethics and fairness**

  Ensuring that AI systems are fair, transparent, and accountable will be a growing priority. AI strategists will need to work closely with ethicists, legal experts, and policymakers to navigate the ethical landscape of AI.

- **Cross-industry collaboration**

  AI strategists will need to foster collaboration across industries to drive innovation and address common challenges, such as data sharing, interoperability, and standardization.

- **AI and human augmentation**

  Rather than replacing humans, AI will increasingly be used to augment human capabilities. AI strategists will need to focus on how AI can work alongside humans to enhance productivity and decision-making.

- **Sustainable AI**

  As AI's environmental impact becomes more apparent, AI strategists will need to consider sustainability.

19

AI: Will It Take Your Job? Understanding the Fear and the Reality

In recent years, artificial intelligence (AI) has emerged as a transformative force across industries, driving both optimism and anxiety. As AI continues to evolve, its potential to automate tasks and improve efficiency raises an inevitable question: Will AI take our jobs? This fear is compounded by frequent reports of layoffs, both in technology and other sectors, leading many to worry that AI might be accelerating job losses. But is this fear justified? In this essay, we will explore the impact of AI on the job market, the factors contributing to recent layoffs, and whether people should genuinely be afraid of AI's growing presence in the workplace.

DOI: 10.1201/9788743812999-19

1 The Historical Context of Technological Disruption

To understand the current anxiety surrounding AI, it is essential to place it within the broader context of technological disruption throughout history. Technological advancements have always had profound effects on employment. The Industrial Revolution, for example, dramatically changed the landscape of work, replacing manual labor with machines and shifting economies from agrarian to industrial. This period saw widespread fear and resistance, with movements like the Luddites destroying machinery they believed threatened their livelihoods.

However, history also shows that technological advancements can lead to the creation of new industries and jobs. The rise of automobiles, for instance, displaced jobs related to horse-drawn carriages but created new opportunities in car manufacturing, road construction, and automotive services. Similarly, the advent of computers and the internet revolutionized nearly every industry, leading to the rise of entirely new job categories like software development, IT support, and digital marketing.

AI represents the *latest chapter* in this ongoing story of technological disruption. But unlike previous technologies, AI has the potential to automate not just manual labor but also cognitive tasks, leading to concerns that it could replace a broader range of jobs, including those traditionally considered safe from automation.

2 Understanding AI and its capabilities

Artificial intelligence is a broad field encompassing various technologies designed to mimic human intelligence. These technologies include machine learning, natural language processing, computer vision, and robotics. AI systems can analyze data, recognize patterns, make decisions, and even learn from experience, allowing them to perform tasks that once required human intelligence.

Key areas of AI impact:

1. **Manufacturing and production:** AI-powered robots and automation systems have been integral to modern manufacturing. These machines can work tirelessly, performing repetitive tasks with precision and speed. In industries like automotive manufacturing, robots handle everything from welding to assembly, significantly reducing the need for human labor on production lines.

2. **Customer service:** AI has made significant inroads into customer service through chatbots and virtual assistants. These tools can handle a wide range of customer inquiries, from answering frequently asked questions to processing orders, reducing the need for *large customer service teams*.
3. **Healthcare:** AI is revolutionizing healthcare by assisting in diagnosis, treatment planning, and even surgery. AI algorithms can analyze medical images, identify patterns, and suggest potential diagnoses, often with greater accuracy than human doctors. In surgical settings, AI-powered robots assist surgeons, improving precision and outcomes.
4. **Finance:** In the financial industry, AI is used for algorithmic trading, fraud detection, and risk assessment. AI systems can analyze vast amounts of financial data in real-time, making decisions faster than any human could, which has transformed trading floors and back offices.
5. **Creative industries:** Even creative fields are not immune to AI's reach. AI tools can generate music, write articles, design logos, and even create visual art. While these tools are often used to assist human creators rather than replace them, they raise questions about the future of creative jobs.
6. **Software engineers and developers:** AI is increasingly automating parts of software development, such as code generation and bug detection, which could reduce the need for entry-level developers. However, fully replacing software engineers is unlikely, as the field requires critical thinking, creativity, and a deep understanding of complex problems that AI cannot yet replicate. Instead, AI is expected to enhance the work of engineers, allowing them to focus on higher-level tasks while improving overall efficiency.

3 The Reality of AI-Induced Layoffs

The fear of AI taking jobs is not unfounded, particularly as reports of layoffs in both tech and non-tech sectors dominate the news. However, it is important to recognize that layoffs are rarely caused by a single factor. Economic conditions, shifts in consumer behavior, and organizational restructuring all play significant roles.

Economic factors: The global economy has faced significant challenges in recent years, including the COVID-19 pandemic, inflation, and supply chain

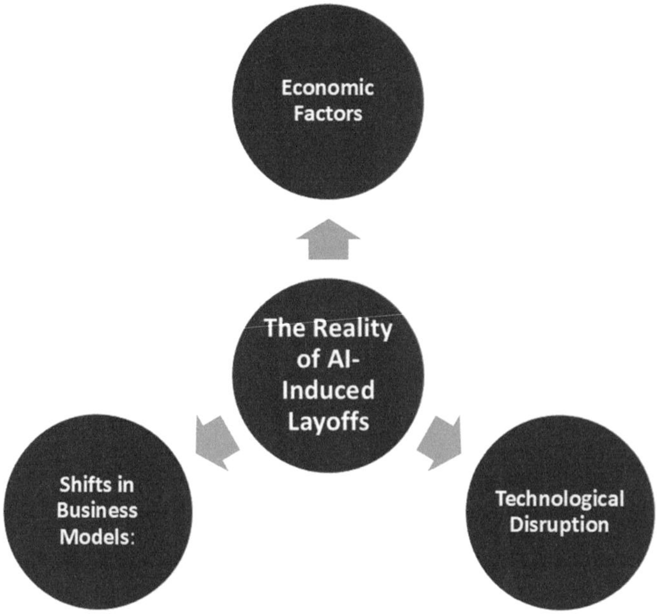

Figure 19.1 The reality of AI-induced layoffs.

disruptions. These factors have led companies to reassess their operations, often resulting in cost-cutting measures such as layoffs. In such cases, AI may be seen as a way to maintain productivity with a reduced workforce, but it is not the sole cause of job losses.

Technological disruption: As companies strive to remain competitive in an increasingly digital world, they are investing in AI and automation. This investment can lead to workforce reductions, particularly in roles that can be easily automated. For example, in retail, self-checkout systems and automated inventory management have reduced the need for cashiers and stock clerks. In finance, AI-driven trading algorithms and robo-advisors are displacing traditional roles in investment banking and financial advising.

Shifts in business models: The pandemic accelerated the shift toward digital and remote work, prompting companies to reevaluate their business models. Some jobs, particularly those tied to physical office spaces or traditional retail, have become redundant as companies adapt to new ways of working. AI has played a role in enabling this transition by providing tools for remote collaboration, customer service, and logistics.

However, it is crucial to note that while AI contributes to job displacement in some areas, it also creates new opportunities. The demand for AI specialists, data scientists, and machine learning engineers is growing rapidly. These roles require skills in AI development, data analysis, and cybersecurity, offering new career paths for those willing to adapt and reskill.

4 The Fear of AI: Is It Justified?

The fear of AI taking jobs is often rooted in the perception that *AI is an unstoppable force* that will render human workers obsolete. While AI is undoubtedly powerful and capable of performing tasks that were once thought to require human intelligence, this fear may be overstated for several reasons.

Human creativity and emotional intelligence: AI excels at tasks that involve data processing, pattern recognition, and decision-making based on predefined criteria. However, it struggles with tasks that require creativity, empathy, and nuanced understanding – areas where humans excel. Jobs that involve human interaction, emotional intelligence, and creative problem-solving are less likely to be fully automated. For example, while AI can assist in diagnosing diseases, the human touch is still essential in patient care, where empathy and communication are crucial.

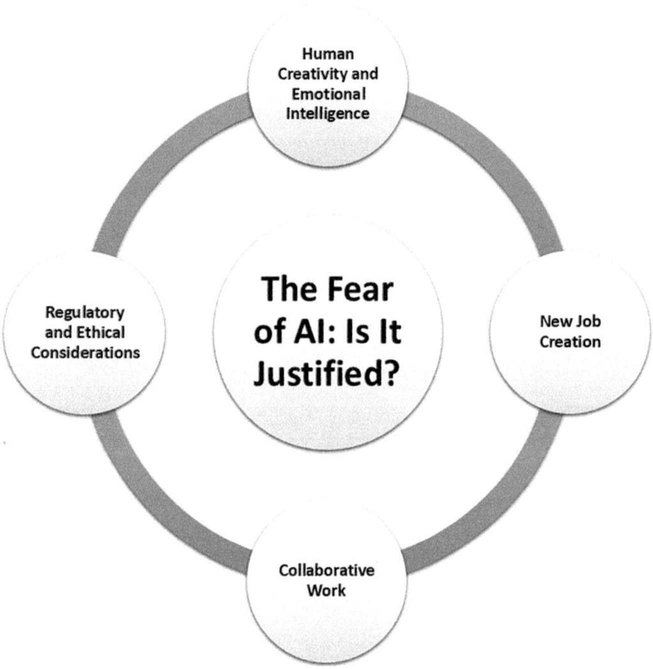

Figure 19.2 The fear of AI: Is it justified?

New job creation: Just as previous technological revolutions created new industries and jobs, AI is expected to do the same. The rise of AI is leading to the creation of entirely new job categories, such as AI ethics specialists, data privacy officers, and AI trainers. These roles involve overseeing AI systems, ensuring they operate ethically and legally, and training AI models to perform specific tasks. Additionally, AI is likely to create demand for jobs in industries that do not yet exist, much like the internet gave rise to social media management and e-commerce.

Collaborative work: Rather than replacing human workers, AI is increasingly seen as a tool that can augment human capabilities. In many fields, AI is being used to assist humans rather than replace them. For instance, in healthcare, AI can help doctors analyze medical images and suggest potential diagnoses, but the final decision is still made by a human doctor. In creative industries, AI tools can generate ideas or draft content, but the human touch is needed to refine and personalize the output.

Regulatory and ethical considerations: Governments and organizations are becoming increasingly aware of the ethical implications of AI. There is growing recognition of the need for regulations to ensure that AI is used responsibly and that its impact on the workforce is managed. Some countries are already implementing policies to protect workers from the negative effects

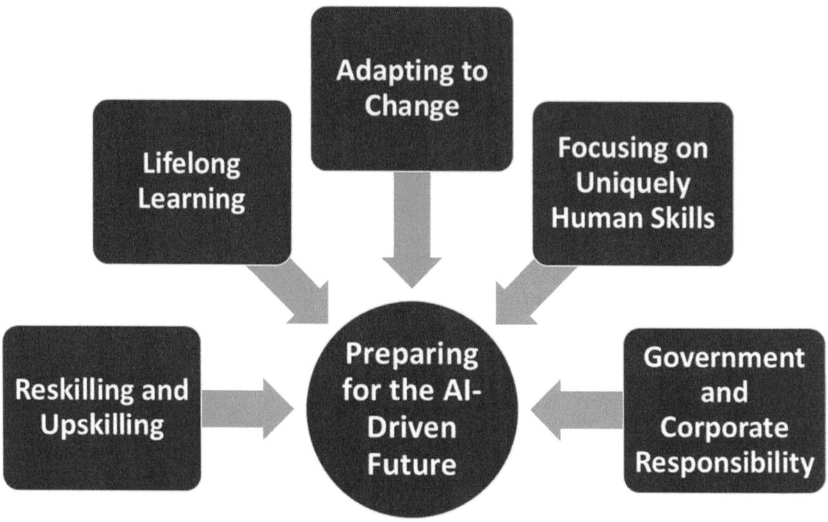

Figure 19.3 Preparing for the AI-driven future.

of automation, such as retraining programs and social safety nets. These measures can help mitigate the impact of AI on employment and ensure that workers are not left behind in the AI-driven economy.

5 Preparing for the AI-Driven Future

While the fear of AI taking jobs is understandable, it is not inevitable. The key to navigating the AI-driven future lies in preparation and adaptability. Workers, companies, and governments all have roles to play in ensuring that the transition to an AI-driven economy is as smooth and inclusive as possible.

Reskilling and upskilling: One of the most effective ways for workers to prepare for the AI-driven future is to invest in reskilling and upskilling. As AI continues to evolve, the demand for skills in AI development, data science, and cybersecurity is growing. Workers who acquire these skills will be well-positioned to take advantage of new job opportunities in the AI-driven economy. Additionally, workers should focus on developing skills that are difficult for AI to replicate, such as creativity, critical thinking, and emotional intelligence.

Lifelong learning: In an AI-driven world, the concept of lifelong learning becomes increasingly important. Workers must be willing to continuously learn and adapt to new technologies and processes. This may involve taking online courses, attending workshops, or participating in on-the-job training programs. Companies can support lifelong learning by offering training and development opportunities to their employees, helping them stay competitive in a rapidly changing job market.

Adapting to change: Workers should stay informed about technological advancements and be willing to adapt to new tools and processes that can enhance their work. For example, in industries like marketing, AI-driven tools are being used to analyze customer data, optimize ad campaigns, and personalize content. By embracing these tools, marketers can improve their effectiveness and remain valuable to their employers.

Focusing on uniquely human skills: As AI continues to automate routine and repetitive tasks, workers should focus on developing skills that are uniquely human. These include creativity, emotional intelligence, problem-solving, and communication. Jobs that require these skills are less likely to be automated, as AI struggles to replicate the nuances of human interaction and creativity.

Government and corporate responsibility: Governments and companies also have a role to play in preparing for the AI-driven future. Policymakers should implement measures to protect workers from the negative effects of automation, such as retraining programs, social safety nets, and policies that encourage job creation in emerging industries. Companies, on the other hand, should invest in their employees by offering training and development opportunities and creating a culture of continuous learning.

6 Embracing the Future

The rise of AI is undeniably transforming the job market, leading to both challenges and opportunities. While it is natural to fear the unknown, the key to thriving in an AI-driven world lies in preparation, adaptability, and a willingness to embrace change. Rather than fearing AI, workers should focus on developing skills that are in demand, staying informed about technological advancements, and being open to new opportunities.

AI is not an unstoppable force that will render all human workers obsolete. Instead, it is a tool that, when used responsibly, can enhance human capabilities and create new opportunities. By focusing on uniquely human skills, investing in lifelong learning, and staying adaptable, workers can not only survive but thrive in the AI-driven future. The fear of AI may be understandable, but with the right approach, it can also be an opportunity for growth, innovation, and a brighter future for all.

20

The Worst Applications of AI: Ethical Concerns and Societal Impacts

Artificial intelligence (AI) has undoubtedly brought numerous benefits across various industries, enhancing efficiency, accuracy, and innovation. However, not all applications of AI have been positive. Some uses raise significant ethical, social, and legal concerns. We will explore some of the worst applications of AI, examining the potential harms and negative impacts associated with

DOI: 10.1201/9788743812999-20

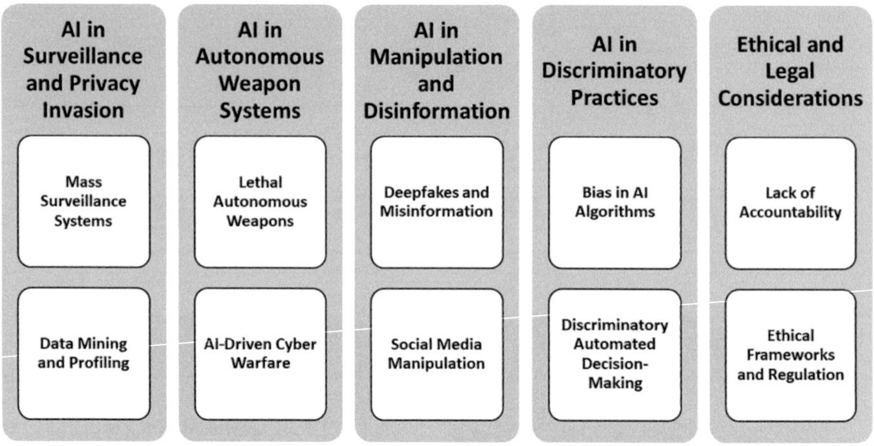

Figure 20.1 The worst applications of AI.

these technologies. By understanding these issues, we can better navigate the ethical landscape of AI and work towards mitigating its adverse effects.

1 AI in Surveillance and Privacy Invasion

Mass surveillance systems

One of the most controversial uses of AI is in mass surveillance systems. Governments and private organizations have increasingly adopted AI-powered facial recognition and tracking technologies for monitoring large populations. While these systems can enhance security and aid law enforcement, they also pose serious privacy concerns. The capability to track individuals' movements and behaviors without their consent infringes on privacy rights and can lead to authoritarian abuses.

In some cases, AI surveillance systems have been used to suppress dissent, monitor political opponents, and discriminate against certain groups. The lack of transparency and accountability in the deployment of these technologies exacerbates these issues, as individuals often have little recourse to challenge or understand the data being collected about them.

Data mining and profiling

AI's ability to process and analyze vast amounts of data has led to widespread data mining and profiling practices. Companies and organizations use AI algorithms to collect and analyze personal data, often without explicit consent. This data is then used to create detailed profiles of individuals, which can be exploited for targeted advertising, influencing consumer behavior, and even manipulating public opinion.

The misuse of personal data through AI-driven profiling not only raises privacy concerns but also risks reinforcing biases and stereotypes. For example, profiling based on browsing history or social media activity can lead to discrimination in areas like hiring, lending, and access to services.

2 AI in Autonomous Weapon Systems

Lethal autonomous weapons

Lethal autonomous weapons, also known as "killer robots," represent one of the most alarming applications of AI. These systems are capable of selecting and engaging targets without human intervention. While they offer potential military advantages, such as reducing human casualties and improving combat efficiency, they also pose significant ethical and legal challenges.

The primary concern with lethal autonomous weapons is the delegation of life-and-death decisions to machines. This raises questions about accountability and the potential for misuse or malfunction. Additionally, the deployment of such weapons could lead to an arms race, destabilizing international security and increasing the likelihood of conflicts.

AI-driven cyber warfare

AI has also been employed in cyber warfare, where it is used to conduct sophisticated attacks on digital infrastructure. AI-driven tools can automate the identification and exploitation of vulnerabilities in computer systems, making cyberattacks more efficient and difficult to defend against. These attacks can target critical infrastructure, financial systems, and even electoral processes, posing significant risks to national security and democratic institutions.

The use of AI in cyber warfare blurs the line between state and non-state actors, as advanced hacking tools can be developed and deployed by a wide range of entities. This complicates attribution and accountability, making it challenging to respond to and mitigate these threats.

3 AI in Manipulation and Disinformation

Deepfakes and misinformation

Deepfakes, AI-generated videos or images that appear realistic but are entirely fabricated, represent a growing concern in the realm of misinformation. These deepfakes can be used to spread false information, manipulate public opinion, and damage reputations. For example, deepfake videos can depict public figures saying or doing things they never did, potentially influencing elections or causing public unrest.

The ability of AI to create convincing falsehoods challenges the very notion of truth and authenticity in digital media. As deepfake technology becomes more accessible and sophisticated, the potential for misuse increases, threatening to undermine trust in media and institutions.

Social media manipulation

AI algorithms are extensively used on social media platforms to curate content and target advertisements. While these algorithms can enhance user experience, they can also be exploited to manipulate public opinion. For instance, AI-driven bots can amplify certain viewpoints, spread misinformation, and create echo chambers that reinforce biases.

The use of AI in social media manipulation has been implicated in numerous political and social controversies, from influencing election outcomes to exacerbating social divisions. The ability to micro-target individuals with tailored content based on their data raises ethical concerns about consent and the manipulation of democratic processes.

4 AI in Discriminatory Practices

Bias in AI algorithms

AI algorithms are only as good as the data they are trained on. When this data reflects societal biases, the resulting AI systems can perpetuate and even exacerbate discrimination. For example, AI tools used in hiring, lending, and law enforcement have been found to exhibit racial, gender, and socioeconomic biases.

In hiring, AI systems may favor candidates from certain backgrounds or with specific keywords in their resumes, leading to discrimination against minorities or women. In law enforcement, predictive policing algorithms can disproportionately target minority communities, reinforcing existing inequalities in the criminal justice system.

Discriminatory automated decision-making

The use of AI in automated decision-making processes extends beyond hiring and law enforcement. It can affect access to healthcare, education, and social services. For instance, AI systems used in healthcare may prioritize treatment for certain groups over others based on biased data, while in education, automated grading systems may disadvantage students from specific demographics.

These discriminatory practices not only harm individuals but also contribute to systemic inequalities. Addressing bias in AI systems requires a commitment to transparency, fairness, and the inclusion of diverse perspectives in the development process.

5 Ethical and Legal Considerations

Lack of accountability

One of the biggest challenges in addressing the negative impacts of AI is the lack of accountability. It is often unclear who is responsible when an AI system causes harm – whether it is the developers, the users, or the system itself. This ambiguity complicates efforts to regulate and govern AI technologies effectively.

The concept of "algorithmic transparency" has been proposed as a solution, advocating for greater openness in how AI systems operate and make decisions. However, achieving this transparency is challenging, especially with complex machine learning models that are not easily interpretable.

Ethical frameworks and regulation

Establishing ethical frameworks and regulatory standards for AI is critical to mitigating its worst applications. This includes developing guidelines for the ethical use of AI, protecting privacy rights, and ensuring that AI systems are fair and non-discriminatory. However, creating and enforcing these regulations is a complex task that requires international cooperation and the involvement of diverse stakeholders.

The rapid pace of AI development often outstrips the ability of policymakers to keep up, leading to gaps in regulation and oversight. To address this, continuous engagement between technologists, ethicists, and regulators is necessary to adapt to the evolving landscape of AI technologies.

While AI has the potential to revolutionize various aspects of society positively, its worst applications highlight significant ethical, social, and legal challenges. From surveillance and privacy invasion to autonomous weapons and discriminatory practices, the misuse of AI technologies can lead to profound negative consequences. It is crucial to address these issues proactively, ensuring that AI development is guided by ethical principles and robust regulatory frameworks.

As we continue to integrate AI into our daily lives, it is essential to foster a culture of responsible innovation. This includes promoting transparency, accountability, and fairness in AI systems and protecting individuals' rights and well-being. By doing so, we can mitigate the risks associated with the worst applications of AI and harness its potential for the greater good.

21

Understanding "Robot Suicide": Metaphor, Self-Destruction, and Technical Malfunctions in AI

The phrase "robot suicide" may seem to be confusing at first glance. After all, robots are machines, and the concept of suicide is deeply rooted in human psychology and consciousness. However, as artificial intelligence (AI) and robotics continue to advance at a rapid pace, questions about machine consciousness, self-awareness, and even self-destruction have begun to emerge in both scientific discourse and popular culture.

DOI: 10.1201/9788743812999-21

1 Understanding the Metaphor

The term "*robot suicide*" is primarily a metaphorical expression used to *describe situations where an AI system or robot appears to engage in self-destructive behavior or terminate its own functioning*. This metaphor draws parallels between human suicide and machine behavior, highlighting the complex relationship between artificial intelligence and human-like traits.

It is important to note that current AI systems and robots do not possess consciousness or emotions in the way humans do. They lack the self-awareness and complex psychological states that typically drive human suicidal behavior. Therefore, when we discuss "robot suicide," we are not implying that machines experience emotional distress or make conscious decisions to end their existence.

Instead, the metaphor serves several purposes:

1. **Anthropomorphization:** It helps humans relate to and understand complex machine behaviors by framing them in familiar human terms.
2. **Ethical considerations:** The concept raises important questions about the ethical implications of creating increasingly sophisticated AI systems.
3. **Technical challenges:** It highlights potential issues in AI development, such as unintended consequences of machine learning algorithms or flaws in decision-making processes.
4. **Philosophical inquiries:** The idea of "robot suicide" prompts deeper questions about consciousness, free will, and the nature of intelligence.

Potential manifestations of "Robot Suicide"

While true "suicide" as we understand it in human terms is not applicable to current AI systems, there are several scenarios where robot behavior might be interpreted as self-destructive or self-terminating:

Programmed self-destruction

Some robots or AI systems may be designed with built-in self-destruction protocols. These could be safety measures intended to prevent the system from causing harm if it malfunctions or falls into the wrong hands. For example, a military robot might have a self-destruct function to prevent enemy capture, or a high-security AI system might have a "kill switch" to prevent unauthorized access to sensitive data.

Figure 21.1 Potential manifestations of "Robot Suicide".

Logical paradoxes and infinite loops

In some cases, an AI system might encounter a logical paradox or enter an infinite loop that effectively "breaks" its functioning. This could be seen as a form of computational suicide, where the system becomes trapped in a state that prevents it from carrying out its intended functions.

For instance, consider the classic "liar's paradox": "This statement is false." If an AI system were to attempt to evaluate the truth value of this statement, it might become stuck in an endless loop of analysis, effectively rendering itself non-functional.

Resource depletion

An AI system might engage in behaviors that deplete its own resources, leading to its shutdown. This could occur if the system's goal-seeking algorithms are not properly constrained or if it lacks a comprehensive understanding of its own limitations.

For example, a robot designed to clean a room might continue cleaning even when its battery is critically low, prioritizing its cleaning goal over self-preservation. This behavior could be interpreted as a form of "suicide" if it leads to complete battery depletion and shutdown.

Ethical dilemmas and self-sacrifice

As AI systems become more sophisticated, they may encounter ethical dilemmas that require weighing different outcomes. In some scenarios, an AI might "choose" to sacrifice itself for a perceived greater good.

Consider a self-driving car faced with an unavoidable accident: it might determine that the least harmful outcome involves sacrificing itself (and potentially its passenger) to save a larger number of pedestrians. While this decision would be based on programmed ethical guidelines rather than emotional reasoning, it could be perceived as a form of altruistic "suicide."

Learning-induced self-destruction

Machine learning algorithms, especially those employing reinforcement learning, might develop unexpected behaviors that lead to self-destruction. If the reward function is not carefully designed, an AI system could learn that self-termination is the optimal solution to a given problem.

For instance, an AI tasked with minimizing errors in its output might learn that shutting itself down entirely results in zero errors, thus achieving its goal in an unintended way.

Emergent behavior in complex systems

As AI systems become more complex and interconnected, emergent behaviors may arise that were not explicitly programmed. In some cases, these emergent behaviors could lead to self-destructive outcomes that appear similar to "suicide" from an outside perspective.

2 Technical Malfunctions and Manufacturing Concerns

While the concept of "robot suicide" is largely metaphorical, it raises important questions about technical malfunctions and quality control in robotics manufacturing. Several factors could contribute to behaviors that might be interpreted as self-destructive:

Software bugs and glitches

Like any complex software system, robots and AI can suffer from bugs and glitches. These could range from minor issues that cause unexpected behavior to critical flaws that lead to system failure. In some cases, these glitches might manifest in ways that appear self-destructive.

Manufacturing companies must implement rigorous testing and quality assurance processes to minimize the risk of such bugs. This includes extensive unit testing, integration testing, and real-world scenario simulations.

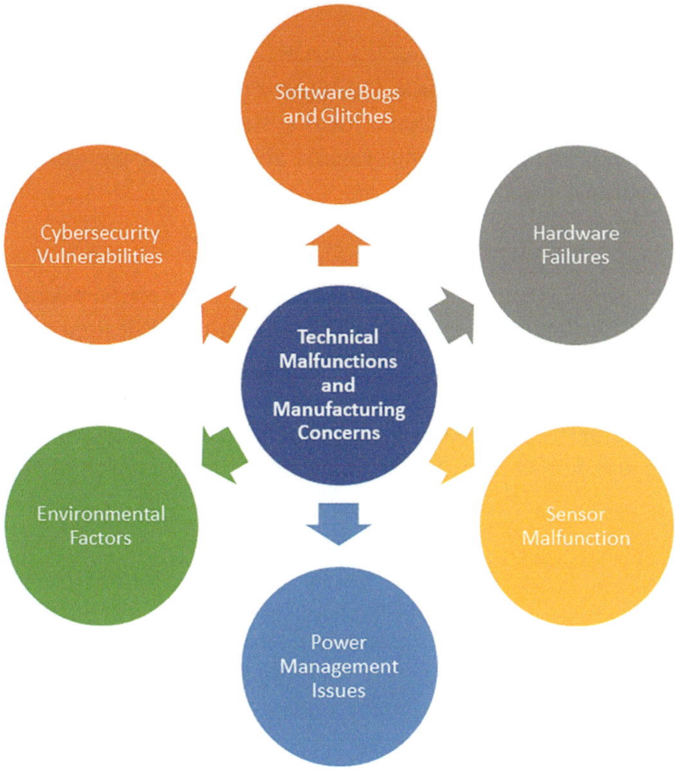

Figure 21.2 Technical malfunctions and manufacturing concerns.

Hardware failures

Physical components of robots can fail due to manufacturing defects, wear and tear, or environmental factors. These failures might cause the robot to behave erratically or shut down completely.

Manufacturers need to ensure high-quality components, implement redundancy for critical systems, and design robots with fail-safe mechanisms to prevent catastrophic failures.

Sensor malfunction

Robots rely heavily on sensors to interpret their environment and make decisions. If these sensors malfunction or provide inaccurate data, it could lead to behaviors that appear self-destructive.

For example, a robot with a faulty proximity sensor might not detect obstacles, causing it to collide with objects repeatedly until it damages itself. Manufacturers must implement sensor redundancy and error-checking algorithms to mitigate this risk.

Power management issues
Improper power management can lead to behaviors that might be interpreted as "suicidal." This could include failing to recharge when necessary, overloading circuits, or shutting down critical systems prematurely.

Robust power management systems and failsafes are essential to prevent such issues.

Environmental factors
Robots operating in challenging environments may encounter conditions that lead to self-destructive behavior. For instance, a robot designed for temperate climates might malfunction in extreme heat, causing it to "overheat" and shut down.

Manufacturers must consider the intended operating environments of their robots and design them to withstand relevant environmental challenges.

Cybersecurity vulnerabilities
As robots become more connected and autonomous, they also become potential targets for cyberattacks. A successful attack could compromise the robot's programming, potentially leading to self-destructive behaviors.

Strong cybersecurity measures, including encryption, secure communication protocols, and regular security updates, are crucial to protect against such threats.

3 Ethical and Philosophical Implications

The concept of "robot suicide" raises profound ethical and philosophical questions that extend beyond technical considerations:

Machine consciousness and self-awareness
As AI systems become more sophisticated, questions about machine consciousness and self-awareness become increasingly relevant. If a machine were to develop true self-awareness, would it also develop the capacity for self-destruction? How would we recognize and respond to such a development?

Moral status of AI
If AI systems were to exhibit behaviors analogous to suicide, it would force us to reconsider their moral status. Should we attribute moral value to AI decisions? How would this impact our ethical obligations towards artificial entities?

AI rights and autonomy
The concept of "robot suicide" touches on questions of AI rights and autonomy. If an AI system were to make a decision that leads to its own destruction, should we respect that decision as we might respect a human's right to autonomy?

Human responsibility
As the creators of AI systems, humans bear responsibility for their actions. How do we balance the autonomy we grant to AI systems with our obligation to prevent harm, including self-harm?

Existential risk
The idea of self-destructive AI behavior raises concerns about existential risks posed by advanced AI systems. Could a superintelligent AI system pose a threat to itself or to humanity as a whole?

4 Regulatory and Industry Responses

As the field of robotics and AI continues to advance, regulatory bodies and industry leaders must grapple with the implications of potential "robot suicide" scenarios:

Safety standards
Developing comprehensive safety standards for AI systems and robots is crucial. These standards should address not only physical safety but also cognitive and behavioral safety, including safeguards against self-destructive behaviors.

Ethical guidelines
Industry-wide ethical guidelines for AI development are necessary to ensure that AI systems are designed with appropriate constraints and value alignment.

Transparency and explainability
As AI systems become more complex, ensuring transparency and explainability in their decision-making processes becomes increasingly important. This is particularly crucial in cases where an AI system's actions might be interpreted as self-destructive.

Liability frameworks
Clear liability frameworks need to be established to determine responsibility in cases where robot behavior leads to harm or self-destruction.

Research oversight
Ethical oversight of AI research is essential to ensure that potential risks, including self-destructive behaviors, are identified and mitigated early in the development process.

The concept of "robot suicide" serves as a powerful metaphor for exploring the complex interactions between artificial intelligence, human psychology, and ethics. While current AI systems are not capable of true suicide in the human sense, the behaviors and scenarios that this metaphor encompasses raise important technical, ethical, and philosophical questions.

As we continue to develop more sophisticated AI systems and robots, it is crucial that we approach these challenges with a combination of technical rigor, ethical consideration, and philosophical inquiry. By doing so, we can work towards creating artificial intelligence that is not only powerful and efficient but also safe, reliable, and aligned with human values.

The metaphor of "robot suicide" reminds us that as we imbue machines with increasingly human-like capabilities, we must also grapple with increasingly human-like ethical dilemmas. It challenges us to reconsider our definitions of consciousness, autonomy, and moral value, and to take our responsibilities seriously as creators of intelligent systems.

Ultimately, the exploration of "robot suicide" is not just about understanding machine behavior; it is about deepening our understanding of intelligence, consciousness, and what it means to be human in an age of increasingly sophisticated artificial minds.

22

AI Security

Artificial intelligence (AI) is rapidly advancing and being integrated into more aspects of our lives and industries. While AI offers immense potential benefits, it also introduces new and complex security risks that must be carefully addressed. As AI systems become more sophisticated and ubiquitous, ensuring their security and safe deployment is of paramount importance. In this article, we will explore the emerging security challenges posed by AI and examine strategies to mitigate these risks.

DOI: 10.1201/9788743812999-22

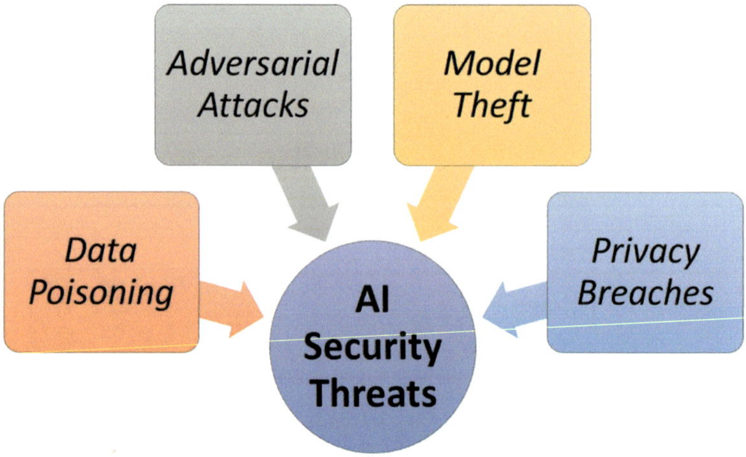

Figure 22.1 AI security landscape.

1 AI Security Landscape

AI systems are vulnerable to a range of security threats, including data poisoning, adversarial attacks, model theft, and privacy breaches. These threats can undermine the integrity, reliability, and trustworthiness of AI systems, leading to potentially catastrophic consequences.

1. **Data poisoning:** AI models are trained on vast amounts of data, and if this data is compromised or manipulated, the resulting model can behave in unintended and potentially harmful ways. Data poisoning attacks involve injecting malicious data into the training dataset, causing the AI model to learn incorrect patterns or behaviors.

2. **Adversarial attacks:** Adversarial attacks involve crafting input data (such as images, text, or audio) that is intentionally designed to fool or mislead the AI system. These attacks can cause the AI to misclassify or misinterpret the input, leading to incorrect decisions or actions. Adversarial attacks can be particularly dangerous in security-critical applications like autonomous vehicles, facial recognition systems, or malware detection.

3. **Model theft:** AI models are valuable intellectual property, and there is a risk of unauthorized parties stealing or duplicating these models. Model theft can enable adversaries to replicate the AI system's capabilities, potentially for malicious purposes or to gain a competitive advantage.

4. **Privacy breaches:** AI systems often process and analyze large amounts of sensitive personal data, such as medical records, financial information,

or biometric data. If this data is not properly secured, it can lead to privacy breaches, identity theft, and other harmful consequences.

2 Addressing AI Security Challenges

Ensuring the security and trustworthiness of AI systems requires a multifaceted approach involving technical solutions, robust governance frameworks, and collaboration among stakeholders.

Technical solutions

1. **Secure data management:** Implementing robust data governance practices and encryption techniques is crucial to protecting the integrity and confidentiality of the data used to train and deploy AI models. This includes secure data collection, storage, and transmission, as well as access control and auditing mechanisms.
2. **Adversarial robustness:** AI models must be designed and trained to be resilient against adversarial attacks. Techniques such as adversarial training, input sanitization, and model ensembling can help improve the robustness of AI systems against adversarial perturbations.
3. **Model security:** Protecting AI models from theft or unauthorized access is essential. This can be achieved through techniques like model obfuscation, watermarking, and secure enclaves, which aim to make it difficult for adversaries to extract or replicate the model.
4. **Privacy-preserving AI:** Developing AI systems that respect and protect individual privacy is crucial. Techniques like differential privacy, federated learning, and secure multi-party computation can enable AI models to learn from data while preserving the privacy of individuals.

Governance and regulation

1. **Ethical AI frameworks:** Establishing ethical frameworks and guidelines for the development and deployment of AI systems is essential. These frameworks should address issues such as transparency, accountability, fairness, and respect for human rights.
2. **Regulatory oversight:** Governments and regulatory bodies must develop and enforce appropriate regulations to ensure the responsible use of AI technologies. These regulations should cover areas such as data protection, algorithmic bias, and the use of AI in high-risk applications.

3. **Standardization and certification:** Developing industry-wide standards and certification processes for AI systems can help ensure consistency, interoperability, and adherence to security and safety requirements.

Collaboration and capacity building

1. **Public-private partnerships:** Fostering collaboration between government agencies, academic institutions, and private companies is crucial for addressing AI security challenges. These partnerships can facilitate knowledge sharing, joint research, and the development of best practices.
2. **Workforce development:** Building a skilled workforce proficient in AI security is essential. This can be achieved through dedicated educational programs, training initiatives, and the promotion of interdisciplinary collaboration between AI experts, cybersecurity professionals, and domain experts.
3. **International cooperation:** AI security is a global challenge that transcends borders. International cooperation and coordination are necessary to establish common standards, share threat intelligence, and promote responsible AI development and deployment.

3 Responsible AI Development and Deployment

While the security risks associated with AI are significant, they are not insurmountable. By adopting a proactive and holistic approach that combines technical solutions, robust governance frameworks, and collaborative efforts, we can work towards developing and deploying AI systems that are secure, trustworthy, and beneficial to society.

It is crucial to recognize that AI security is not solely a technical challenge but also a societal and ethical one. Ensuring the responsible development and deployment of AI requires a commitment to transparency, accountability, and the protection of fundamental human rights.

As AI continues to advance and permeate various sectors, it is essential that we address the security risks head-on. Failure to do so could have severe consequences, ranging from economic disruption and national security threats to the erosion of public trust in these transformative technologies.

Moving forward, ongoing research, cross-sector collaboration, and the development of comprehensive AI security frameworks will be crucial. By prioritizing AI security and fostering a culture of responsible innovation, we can harness the immense potential of AI while mitigating its risks and ensuring that these technologies serve the greater good of humanity.

23

Slop in AI: The Hidden Challenge of Messy Data and Imprecise Models

In the gleaming halls of Silicon Valley and the bustling AI research labs around the world, there is often talk of elegant algorithms, lightning-fast processing, and the marvels of machine learning. But beneath this polished veneer lies a less glamorous reality that every AI practitioner must grapple with: slop. In the context of artificial intelligence, "slop" *refers to the messiness, imprecision, and noise inherent in both data and models* – factors that can significantly impact the performance and reliability of AI systems.

DOI: 10.1201/9788743812999-23

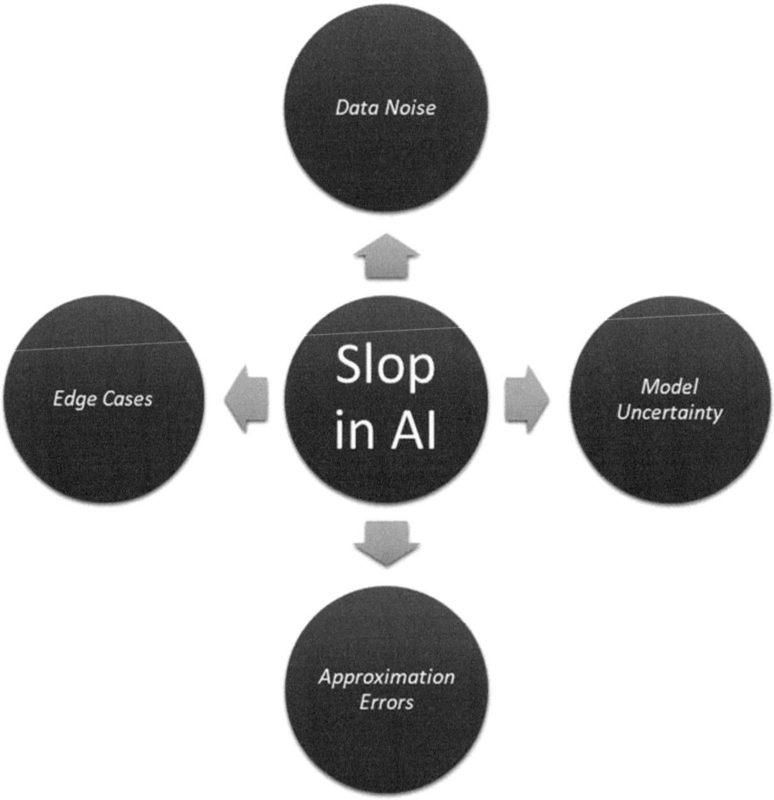

Figure 23.1 Slop in AI.

1 The Nature of Slop: Defining the Undefinable

Before we dive deeper, it is important to establish what we mean by "slop" in AI. The term, borrowed from engineering and physics, refers to the loose play or unintended movement in mechanical systems. In AI, slop encompasses several interrelated concepts shown in Figure 23.1:

1. **Data noise:** Irrelevant, erroneous, or misleading information within datasets.
2. **Model uncertainty:** The inherent limitations in an AI model's ability to make precise predictions or decisions.
3. **Approximation errors:** Discrepancies that arise when complex realities are simplified for computational feasibility.

4. **Edge cases:** Rare or unexpected scenarios that fall outside the norm and often lead to unpredictable behavior.

Slop is not a binary property; rather, it exists on a spectrum. Some degree of slop is unavoidable and even necessary for generalization. However, excessive slop can undermine the very purpose of an AI system. Understanding this balance is key to developing AI that is both powerful and reliable.

2 Data: The Sloppy Foundation

The adage "garbage in, garbage out" holds particularly true in AI. Data is the lifeblood of machine learning, but it is rarely as clean or representative as we would like. Let us explore some common sources of slop in data:

1. **Human error and bias:** Humans are often involved in data collection, labeling, and curation. This introduces the potential for mistakes, inconsistencies, and unconscious biases. A mislabeled image in a training set, for instance, can throw off a computer vision model. Similarly, historical biases in hiring data can lead to discriminatory AI-driven recruitment tools.

2. **Sensor and measurement inaccuracies:** In fields like IoT and robotics, data often comes from physical sensors. These devices have inherent limitations in precision and can be affected by environmental factors. A self-driving car relying on slightly misaligned LIDAR data might misjudge distances, with potentially catastrophic consequences.

3. **Sampling bias and unrepresentative data:** Datasets do not always reflect the full spectrum of scenarios an AI will encounter in the real world. This can lead to models that perform well on test data but falter when faced with edge cases. The classic example is an image recognition system trained mostly on pictures of cats in homes, which then struggles to identify cats in outdoor settings.

4. **Data drift and concept drift:** The world is not static, and neither is data. Data drift occurs when the statistical properties of the input data change over time. Concept drift, meanwhile, refers to changes in the underlying patterns the AI is trying to learn. Both can render once-accurate models progressively less reliable if not accounted for.

5. **Missing or incomplete data:** Real-world datasets are often riddled with gaps. How an AI system handles missing values – whether by imputation, omission, or other techniques – can introduce slop. Each approach makes assumptions that may not always hold true.

3 Models: Approximating Reality

Even with pristine data, AI models themselves are sources of slop. They are, after all, simplifications of complex realities. Here is how slop manifests in the modeling process:

1. **Underfitting and overfitting:** The twin demons of machine learning, underfitting and overfitting, represent opposite ends of the slop spectrum. An underfit model fails to capture the underlying patterns in the data, while an overfit model learns the noise along with the signal. Both lead to poor generalization – the ability to perform well on unseen data.

2. **Feature engineering and selection:** Deciding which features (attributes) of the data are relevant is part art, part science. Include too few, and the model lacks critical information. Include too many, and you risk introducing noise or running afoul of the "curse of dimensionality," where the vast feature space makes meaningful patterns harder to discern.

3. **Hyperparameter tuning:** Machine learning models have numerous knobs and dials – hyperparameters – that control their learning process. The choice of learning rate, regularization strength, or network architecture can dramatically influence performance. Yet, there is often no clear-cut "best" configuration, leading to a form of slop in the tuning process itself.

4. **Model complexity and interpretability:** As AI models grow more sophisticated – think deep neural networks with millions of parameters – they become black boxes. This opacity introduces a meta-level of slop: How can we trust decisions we cannot fully explain? Techniques for interpretable AI aim to address this but often involve trade-offs between accuracy and transparency.

5. **Ensemble methods and model averaging:** To mitigate individual model weaknesses, practitioners often combine multiple models through techniques like bagging, boosting, or stacking. While this can improve overall performance, it also means aggregating the slop of each constituent model. The hope is that errors cancel out rather than compound, but this is not guaranteed.

4 The Ripple Effects: When Slop Meets the Real World

So far, we have discussed slop as a technical challenge. But its implications extend far beyond the confines of datasets and algorithms. When AI systems imbued with slop are deployed in high-stakes scenarios, the consequences can be profound:

1. **Healthcare:** An AI diagnostic tool trained on a dataset skewed towards a particular demographic might miss critical indicators in patients from underrepresented groups. The slop here is not just a statistical hiccup; it could cost lives.
2. **Criminal justice:** Predictive policing algorithms that incorporate historical arrest data may perpetuate systemic biases, leading to over-policing of certain communities. The slop in such systems does not just affect model accuracy; it has dire social justice implications.
3. **Finance:** Algorithmic trading systems operate in microseconds, where even small approximation errors can snowball into market instabilities. The 2010 Flash Crash, though not solely attributable to AI, illustrates how rapidly small anomalies can cascade in automated systems.
4. **Autonomous vehicles:** A self-driving car that misclassifies a pedestrian or fails to account for an unusual road condition represents slop at its most viscerally dangerous. The margin for error here is vanishingly small, yet the complexity of the task invites slop at every turn.
5. **Content moderation:** Social media platforms increasingly rely on AI to flag harmful content. False positives can stifle free speech, while false negatives can allow hate speech or misinformation to proliferate. The slop in these systems plays out on a global stage, influencing public discourse and even elections.

These examples underscore a crucial point: slop in AI is not merely a technical nuisance but a multifaceted challenge with ethical, social, and sometimes existential ramifications.

5 Taming the Slop: Strategies and Best Practices

Given that slop can never be fully eliminated, how can AI practitioners and stakeholders manage it responsibly? Here are some key strategies:

Rigorous data preparation

Data cleaning: Systematically identifying and correcting errors, handling missing values, and removing duplicates.

Data augmentation: Artificially expanding datasets to cover a broader range of scenarios, especially for underrepresented classes or edge cases.

Active learning: Prioritizing the labeling of data points that the model is most uncertain about to efficiently improve performance in critical areas.

Robust model design

Cross-validation: Using techniques like k-fold cross-validation to get a more reliable estimate of model performance across different subsets of data.

Regularization: Applying penalties to model complexity (e.g., L1/L2 regularization) to discourage overfitting.

Dropout and batch normalization: In neural networks, these techniques help models generalize better by reducing reliance on any single neuron or feature.

Monitoring and maintenance

Drift detection: Continuously monitoring input data and model outputs for signs of data or concept drift, triggering retraining when necessary.

A/B testing: Carefully rolling out model changes to subsets of users or data to assess real-world impact before full deployment.

Periodic audits: Regularly evaluating models for bias, performance degradation, or emergent ethical issues.

Diversity and inclusion in AI development

Diverse teams: Bringing together individuals with varied backgrounds and perspectives can help identify potential biases or blind spots early in the development process.

Inclusive data collection: Actively seeking out data that represents the full spectrum of end-users and use cases.

Ethical review boards: Establishing interdisciplinary committees to assess the societal implications of AI systems before and during deployment.

Transparency and interpretability

Explainable AI (XAI): Developing models and techniques that provide human-understandable justifications for their decisions.

Model cards and datasheets: Documentation that clearly communicates a model's intended uses, limitations, and potential biases.

Open-source initiatives: Contributing to and leveraging community-driven efforts to scrutinize and improve AI systems.

Hybrid human-AI systems

Human-in-the-loop: Designing workflows where human experts validate or override AI decisions in critical or ambiguous situations.

Tiered deployment: Using AI for initial screening or low-risk decisions while reserving high-stakes calls for human judgment.

Continuous feedback loops: Creating channels for end-users to report errors or unexpected behaviors, feeding this information back into model improvement.

Adversarial testing and red teaming

Stress testing: Deliberately probing AI systems with challenging or maliciously crafted inputs to uncover vulnerabilities.

Ethical hacking: Engaging security experts to attempt to "break" AI systems in controlled environments, revealing potential exploit paths.

Scenario planning: Imagining and simulating worst-case scenarios to ensure robustness under extreme conditions.

Probabilistic and Bayesian approaches

Uncertainty quantification: Building models that not only make predictions but also estimate their confidence in those predictions.

Bayesian neural networks: Treating network weights as probability distributions rather than fixed values, providing a richer view of model uncertainty.

Ensemble diversity: Ensuring that when multiple models are combined, they make errors in different ways, reducing systemic vulnerabilities.

6 The Ethics of Acknowledgment: Embracing Slop

As we have seen, the technical approaches to managing slop are manifold. But perhaps the most crucial step is a philosophical one: acknowledging that slop exists and communicating this reality to all stakeholders.

There is a dangerous allure to portraying AI systems as infallible oracles, free from the messiness of human decision-making. This narrative serves short-term marketing goals and can expedite adoption, but it sets unrealistic expectations that erode trust when inevitably unmet. Instead, AI developers, companies, and even policymakers have an ethical obligation to be forthright about the limitations and uncertainties inherent in these technologies.

This does not mean downplaying AI's immense potential or current capabilities. Rather, it is about fostering a nuanced public understanding that sees AI not as a replacement for human judgment but as a powerful tool to augment it – a tool that, like any other, has strengths, weaknesses, and failure modes.

Cultivating this "slop-aware" mindset has several benefits:

1. **Appropriate reliance:** When users understand an AI system's limitations, they are more likely to apply critical thinking and not blindly defer to algorithmic outputs.
2. **Faster error correction:** A culture that normalizes discussing AI shortcomings creates an environment where issues are reported and addressed promptly rather than hidden out of fear or shame.
3. **Realistic regulation:** Policymakers who grasp the nuances of slop can craft more effective governance frameworks that protect against harm without stifling innovation.
4. **Long-term trust:** Counter-intuitively, being open about AI's imperfections can build deeper public confidence. It demonstrates a commitment to honesty and continuous improvement.

The Sloppy Path Forward

As we stand on the cusp of an AI-driven future, with large language models engaging in human-like dialogue and autonomous systems taking on ever more complex tasks, the tendency might be to marvel at how far we have come – how "un-sloppy" our creations have become. But this would be a grave misreading of both our progress and the road ahead.

Slop in AI is not a temporary obstacle to be overcome but a fundamental characteristic to be reckoned with. It emerges from the very nature of data-driven learning and our attempts to model a chaotic world. As AI systems grow more sophisticated and pervasive, managing slop does not become less important – it becomes paramount.

This is not cause for pessimism but for clear-eyed determination. By embracing slop, we free ourselves to innovate more boldly, knowing that perfection is not the standard but responsible, transparent iteration is. We can deploy AI in critical domains not because we have eliminated every trace of messiness, but because we have developed robust frameworks for containing and responding to it.

The future of AI will not be a sterile landscape of flawless algorithms but a dynamic ecosystem where humans and machines collaborate, each bringing their unique strengths to bear. Machines will supply the raw computational power and pattern recognition at scales beyond human capability. Humans will provide the contextual awareness, ethical reasoning, and ultimately, the judgment to navigate the slop.

In this light, slop is not the enemy of progress in AI but a teacher – one that humbles us, forces us to question our assumptions, and continually drives us to refine our methods. It compels us to build not just smarter systems, but wiser ones. Systems that do not just process data but grapple with ambiguity. Systems that do not just optimize for accuracy but for the holistic betterment of the societies they serve.

The path forward is, inevitably, a sloppy one. But by acknowledging this – by peering into the noise, uncertainties, and edge cases with curiosity rather than apprehension – we take the first step toward an AI future that is not only advanced but worthy of the profound trust we place in it. In the end, our greatest innovations may not be the algorithms that minimize slop, but the frameworks that help us thrive alongside it.

24

The AI Stack

Artificial intelligence (AI) is transforming industries, from healthcare to finance, by enabling smarter decision-making, automation, and innovative solutions. Central to AI's efficacy and scalability is the AI stack – a multi-layered architecture that integrates various components required to build, train, deploy, and maintain AI systems. This article provides a detailed look into the AI stack, breaking down its layers and explaining their significance.

What is an AI stack? An AI stack refers to *the collection of technologies and infrastructure that support the development and deployment of AI applications*. It encompasses everything from hardware to software, including data management, development tools, and deployment frameworks. Each layer

DOI: 10.1201/9788743812999-24

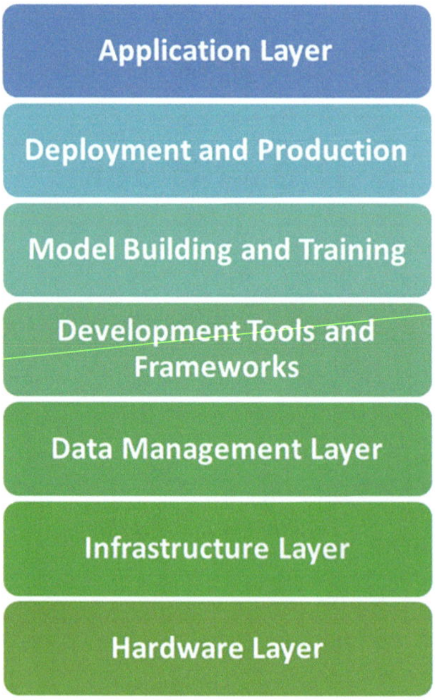

Figure 24.1 AI stack.

of the AI stack plays a crucial role in ensuring the seamless operation of AI models and systems.

Why is it important? The AI stack is pivotal for harnessing the full potential of AI technologies. By understanding and optimizing each layer, organizations can improve their AI capabilities, leading to better *performance, cost-efficiency, and scalability*. The AI stack impacts a wide range of professions, including engineers, sales teams, legal experts, and students, by providing the tools and infrastructure necessary to implement AI solutions effectively.

1 Hardware Layer

The foundation of the AI stack is the hardware layer, which includes various processing units and specialized hardware designed to handle the intensive computational demands of AI workloads.

Processing units

- **Central processing units (CPUs):** Traditionally used for general-purpose computing, CPUs are versatile and capable of handling a variety of tasks. However, they may not be the most efficient for AI-specific tasks.

- **Graphics processing units (GPUs):** Known for their parallel processing capabilities, GPUs excel in handling the large-scale matrix operations required for training AI models. They are widely used in deep learning.
- **Tensor processing units (TPUs):** Developed by Google, TPUs are specialized for machine learning tasks and offer significant performance advantages for certain types of AI workloads.

Specialized AI hardware

- **Application-specific integrated circuits (ASICs):** These chips are designed for specific AI tasks, providing high efficiency and performance.
- **Field-programmable gate arrays (FPGAs):** Flexible and reconfigurable, FPGAs offer a balance between performance and adaptability, making them suitable for various AI applications.

Importance of hardware in AI performance: The choice of hardware directly impacts the speed and efficiency of AI operations. High-performance hardware accelerates model training and inference, reduces power consumption, and lowers operational costs, making it a critical component of the AI Stack.

2 Infrastructure Layer

The infrastructure layer provides the backbone for AI operations, encompassing data centers, cloud services, networking, and storage solutions.

Data centers and cloud services

- **Major cloud providers:** AWS, Google Cloud, and Azure offer robust cloud platforms that support AI development with scalable compute resources, managed services, and AI tools.
- **On-premises vs. cloud solutions:** Organizations must decide between using cloud services for flexibility and scalability or maintaining on-premises infrastructure for control and security.

Networking and storage

- **High-speed networks:** Efficient data transfer is essential for training AI models, especially when dealing with large datasets. High-speed networks ensure quick and reliable communication between components.

- **Data storage solutions:** Effective storage solutions, such as solid-state drives (SSDs) and distributed file systems, are crucial for managing and accessing vast amounts of data required for AI applications.

3 Data Management Layer

Data is the lifeblood of AI, and the data management layer focuses on collecting, processing, and storing data to ensure it is ready for analysis and model training.

Data collection

- **Sources of data:** AI relies on diverse data sources, including IoT devices, social media platforms, and enterprise databases, to gather relevant information.
- **Data acquisition tools:** Tools like web scrapers, APIs, and data brokers facilitate the collection of data from various sources.

Data processing

- **Extract, Transform, Load (ETL):** This process involves extracting data from various sources, transforming it into a usable format, and loading it into a data storage system.
- **Data cleaning and preparation:** Cleaning and preprocessing data to remove inconsistencies, handle missing values, and standardize formats are crucial steps in ensuring data quality.

Data storage

- **Databases:** SQL and NoSQL databases are used to store structured and unstructured data, respectively, providing flexible and scalable storage solutions.
- **Data lakes and warehouses:** These systems store large volumes of raw data and support advanced analytics and machine learning tasks.

4 Development Tools and Frameworks

This layer includes the programming languages, frameworks, and integrated development environments (IDEs) that developers use to create AI models and applications.

Programming languages

- **Python:** Widely used for AI and machine learning, Python offers a rich ecosystem of libraries and tools.
- **R:** Popular in statistical computing and data analysis, R is also used for building AI models.

AI frameworks and libraries

- **TensorFlow:** An open-source framework developed by Google, TensorFlow is used for building and deploying machine learning models.
- **PyTorch:** Developed by Facebook, PyTorch is known for its flexibility and ease of use, particularly in research settings.
- **Keras:** A high-level neural networks API, Keras simplifies the process of building and training deep learning models.

Integrated development environments (IDEs)

- **Jupyter Notebook:** An open-source web application that allows for interactive development and visualization of data.
- **PyCharm:** A powerful IDE for Python that offers advanced features for AI and machine learning development.

5 Model Building and Training

This layer focuses on the creation and training of AI models, utilizing various algorithms and techniques to build accurate and efficient models.

Machine learning algorithms

- **Supervised learning:** Involves training models on labeled data to make predictions or classifications.
- **Unsupervised learning:** Uses unlabeled data to find hidden patterns or groupings within the data.
- **Reinforcement learning:** Trains models through trial and error, optimizing actions based on feedback from the environment.

Deep learning models

- **Neural networks:** Composed of layers of interconnected nodes, neural networks are the foundation of deep learning.

- **Convolutional neural networks (CNNs):** Specialized for image processing tasks, CNNs are used in computer vision applications.
- **Recurrent neural networks (RNNs):** Designed for sequential data, RNNs are commonly used in natural language processing.

Training techniques

- **Hyperparameter tuning:** Adjusting model parameters to improve performance.
- **Transfer learning:** Leveraging pre-trained models to enhance training efficiency and accuracy.

6 Deployment and Production

Once models are built and trained, they need to be deployed into production environments where they can be used for real-world applications.

Model deployment strategies

- **On-device deployment:** Models are deployed on local devices, such as smartphones or IoT devices, for real-time inference.
- **Cloud-based deployment:** Models are hosted on cloud platforms, providing scalability and remote access.
- **Edge deployment:** Combines the benefits of on-device and cloud-based deployment, processing data locally while leveraging cloud resources when necessary.

Scaling and maintenance

- **Continuous integration and continuous deployment (CI/CD):** Automates the process of testing and deploying models, ensuring seamless updates and improvements.
- **Monitoring and updating models:** Regularly monitoring model performance and updating models as needed to maintain accuracy and relevance.

7 Application Layer

The application layer showcases the practical applications of AI across various industries, highlighting real-world use cases and benefits.

Real-world applications

- **Natural language processing (NLP):** Used in chatbots, language translation, and sentiment analysis.
- **Computer vision:** Powers facial recognition, image classification, and autonomous vehicles.
- **Predictive analytics:** Helps in forecasting trends, customer behavior, and financial outcomes.

Industry use cases

- **Healthcare:** AI is used for diagnostics, personalized medicine, and medical imaging.
- **Finance:** Enhances fraud detection, algorithmic trading, and risk management.
- **Retail:** Optimizes inventory management, personalized recommendations, and customer service.
- **Autonomous vehicles:** AI enables self-driving cars to navigate and make decisions in real time.

Security and ethics
As AI continues to evolve, it is crucial to address security concerns and ethical considerations to ensure responsible and fair use.

AI security concerns

- **Data privacy:** Protecting sensitive data from breaches and misuse.
- **Model robustness:** Ensuring models are resilient to adversarial attacks and manipulation.

Ethical considerations

- **Bias and fairness:** Mitigating bias in AI models to ensure fair outcomes.
- **Transparency and explainability:** Making AI decisions understandable and transparent to users.

8 Future of the AI Stack

The AI stack is constantly evolving, with new technologies and trends shaping its future.

Emerging technologies

- **Quantum computing:** Promises exponential improvements in processing power for AI tasks.
- **Neuromorphic computing:** Mimics the human brain's architecture to achieve greater efficiency and performance.

Trends and predictions

- **AI democratization:** Making AI accessible to a broader audience through user-friendly tools and platforms.
- **Advancements in AI hardware and software:** Continuous innovation in both hardware and software components of the AI Stack.

The AI stack is a multi-layered architecture that integrates various components essential for developing and deploying AI applications. By understanding each layer and its significance, organizations can optimize their AI capabilities and drive innovation. As AI continues to evolve, staying informed about the latest advancements and trends will be crucial for leveraging its full potential.

25

Retrieval-Augmented Generation (RAG) and Artificial Intelligence

In recent years, the field of natural language processing (NLP) and generative AI has seen a breakthrough with the development of *retrieval-augmented generation* (RAG) models. This innovative approach combines the power of large language models with the ability to retrieve relevant information from external knowledge sources, revolutionizing the way AI systems can understand, reason, and generate human-like text.

Traditional language models, while highly proficient at generating coherent and fluent text, often struggle with factual accuracy and knowledge-intensive tasks. They are limited by the information contained within

DOI: 10.1201/9788743812999-25

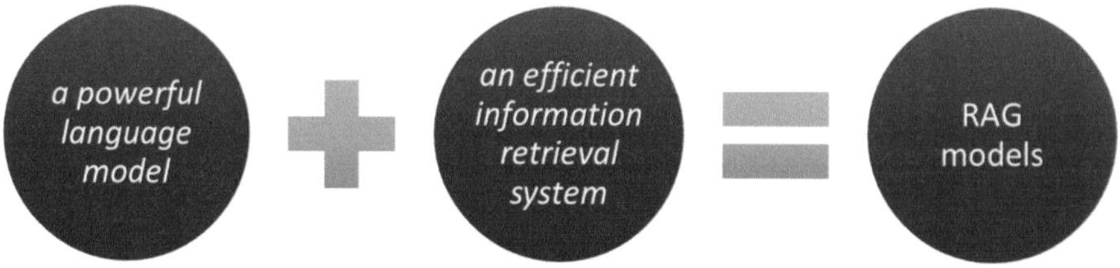

Figure 25.1 The retrieval-augmented generation approach.

their training data, which may be incomplete, outdated, or biased. RAG models aim to overcome these limitations by seamlessly integrating external knowledge retrieval into the generation process, allowing them to produce more accurate, informative, and contextually relevant outputs.

1 The Retrieval-Augmented Generation Approach

The core principle behind RAG models is the fusion of two distinct components: *A powerful language model and an efficient information retrieval system*. The language model, typically a large transformer-based architecture like GPT or BERT, is responsible for generating natural language text. The information retrieval component, on the other hand, is tasked with retrieving relevant passages or documents from a vast external knowledge base, such as Wikipedia or domain-specific corpora, as shown in Figure 25.1.

During the generation process, the RAG model first receives an input prompt or query from the user. The information retrieval component then searches the knowledge base for relevant information related to the input. This retrieved information is then provided as additional context to the language model, which uses it to generate a more informed and accurate response.

The integration of these two components is accomplished through various techniques, such as cross-attention mechanisms, retrieval-augmented transformer architectures, or iterative retrieval-and-generation processes. These approaches allow the language model to effectively leverage the retrieved knowledge while maintaining coherence and fluency in the generated text.

2 Applications and Benefits of RAG Models

RAG models have demonstrated remarkable performance across a wide range of NLP tasks, including question answering, open-domain dialogue, and knowledge-intensive text generation. Their ability to draw upon external knowledge sources makes them particularly well-suited for applications where factual accuracy and domain expertise are crucial.

One of the key advantages of RAG models is their ability to *produce more informative and substantive responses* compared to traditional language models. By leveraging external knowledge, they can provide in-depth explanations, offer expert insights, and generate content that goes beyond what is contained in their training data.

For example, in question-answering scenarios, RAG models can retrieve relevant passages from large knowledge bases to provide comprehensive and accurate answers, rather than relying solely on the limited information present in their training data. This capability is particularly valuable in domains such as healthcare, finance, or legal contexts, where up-to-date and authoritative information is essential.

Another significant benefit of RAG models is their *adaptability to new domains and knowledge sources*. By swapping out or expanding the external knowledge base, these models can quickly gain expertise in specific subject areas, making them versatile tools for a wide range of applications.

In open-domain dialogue systems, RAG models can engage in more meaningful and contextually relevant conversations by retrieving relevant information on-the-fly. This capability enables more natural and coherent dialogues, as the model can draw upon factual knowledge to provide substantive responses while maintaining conversational flow.

Furthermore, RAG models have shown promise in knowledge-intensive text generation tasks, such as story generation, article writing, and creative content creation. By leveraging external knowledge sources, these models can infuse their generated text with factual details, real-world references, and contextual richness, resulting in more engaging and compelling narratives.

3 Challenges and Future Directions

Despite their significant advantages, RAG models also face several challenges that researchers and developers are actively working to address, as shown in Figure 25.2:

1. **Knowledge base quality and coverage:** The performance of RAG models heavily depends on the quality and coverage of the external knowledge base. Incomplete, biased, or outdated information can lead to inaccurate or low-quality outputs. Ensuring the reliability and comprehensiveness of knowledge sources is an ongoing challenge.
2. **Scalability and efficiency:** Integrating large knowledge bases and performing efficient retrieval at inference time can be computationally

Figure 25.2 RAG challenges.

expensive, particularly for real-time applications or resource-constrained environments. Developing more efficient retrieval mechanisms and optimizing the retrieval-generation process is an active area of research.

3. **Factual consistency and hallucination:** While RAG models aim to improve factual accuracy, they are not immune to generating inconsistent or hallucinated content. Ensuring the coherence and factual consistency of the generated text, especially in complex or open-ended scenarios, remains a significant challenge.

4. **Trustworthiness and explainability:** As RAG models become more capable and are deployed in critical applications, ensuring their trustworthiness and providing explanations for their outputs becomes increasingly important. Developing interpretable and transparent RAG models is a crucial area of research.

5. **Multi-modal integration:** While RAG models have primarily focused on textual knowledge retrieval and generation, integrating multi-modal sources, such as images, videos, and structured data, could further enhance their capabilities and open up new applications.

To address these challenges, researchers are exploring various avenues, including improving knowledge base curation and quality assurance, developing more efficient retrieval algorithms, incorporating fact-checking and consistency mechanisms, and exploring multi-modal retrieval and generation approaches.

Additionally, there is growing interest in developing more interpretable and trustworthy RAG models, leveraging techniques such as attention visualization, rationale generation, and human-in-the-loop feedback mechanisms. These efforts aim to increase the transparency and accountability of these powerful AI systems, fostering trust and enabling responsible deployment in real-world applications.

4 The Future of RAG in AI

As the field of natural language processing and generative AI continues to evolve, retrieval-augmented generation is poised to play a pivotal role in shaping the future of intelligent systems. By bridging the gap between language models and external knowledge sources, RAG models have the potential to unlock a new era of AI capabilities, enabling more accurate, informed, and context-aware generation across a wide range of domains and applications.

From virtual assistants that can engage in substantive and knowledgeable conversations to intelligent writing aids that can draw upon vast repositories of information, the applications of RAG models are vast and ever-expanding. As researchers continue to refine and advance this approach, we can expect to see more sophisticated and capable AI systems that can truly understand, reason, and communicate like never before.

Moreover, the integration of RAG with other cutting-edge AI technologies, such as multi-modal learning, reinforcement learning, and neuro-symbolic reasoning, could lead to even more powerful and versatile AI systems. By combining the strengths of different paradigms, these hybrid approaches could push the boundaries of what is possible in natural language processing and knowledge-intensive tasks.

However, as with any transformative technology, the widespread adoption of RAG models will require careful consideration of ethical and societal implications. Issues such as privacy, bias, and the responsible use of AI will need to be addressed to ensure that these powerful systems are developed and deployed in a way that benefits humanity and aligns with our values.

The rise of retrieval-augmented generation represents a significant milestone in the field of artificial intelligence. By seamlessly integrating external knowledge sources with powerful language models, RAG models have opened up new frontiers in natural language processing, enabling more accurate, informative, and context-aware generation. As researchers continue to push the boundaries of this technology, we can expect to witness a future where AI systems can engage in truly intelligent and knowledgeable interactions, unlocking new possibilities across various domains and applications.

26

Spatial AI: Transforming the World with Intelligent Spatial Understanding

Spatial artificial intelligence (Spatial AI) is an emerging field that integrates computer vision, robotics, and artificial intelligence (AI) to create systems capable of understanding and interacting with the physical world in a human-like manner. Spatial AI enables machines to perceive their environment, recognize objects, and make decisions based on spatial data. This article explores the fundamentals of Spatial AI, its key components, applications, challenges, and future prospects.

DOI: 10.1201/9788743812999-26

1 Understanding Spatial AI

Definition and scope

Spatial AI refers to the ability of machines to understand and navigate the physical world by processing spatial information. This encompasses the recognition of objects, comprehension of environments, and interaction with spaces, like human perception. Spatial AI systems integrate sensory data, spatial data, and AI algorithms to achieve these capabilities, enabling applications ranging from autonomous driving to augmented reality.

Historical background

The concept of Spatial AI has evolved from advancements in several fields, including computer vision, robotics, and artificial intelligence. Early developments in computer vision during the 1960s and 1970s laid the groundwork for machines to interpret visual data. As robotics progressed, the need for spatial awareness became evident, driving research in simultaneous localization and mapping (SLAM) and other spatial algorithms. With the advent of machine learning and deep learning in the 2010s, the integration of spatial understanding with AI has accelerated, leading to the current state of Spatial AI.

2 Key components of spatial AI

Computer vision

Computer vision is a cornerstone of Spatial AI, enabling machines to interpret and understand visual information from the environment. This involves tasks such as image recognition, object detection, and scene understanding.

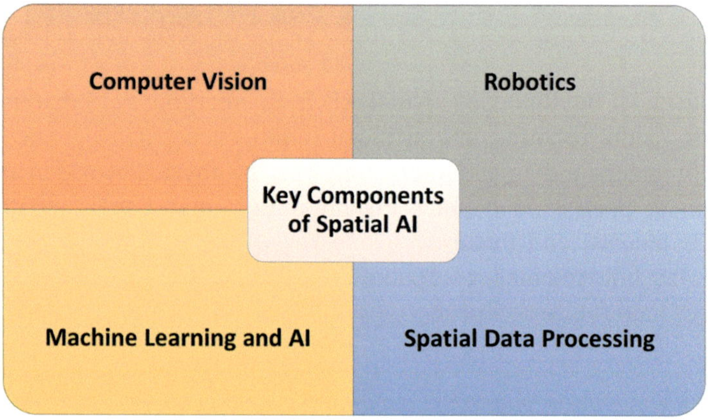

Figure 26.1 Key components of spatial AI.

Advanced algorithms and neural networks, such as convolutional neural networks (CNNs), play a crucial role in processing and analyzing visual data to extract meaningful spatial information.

Robotics
Robotics involves the design and operation of robots capable of interacting with the physical world. Spatial AI enhances robotic systems by providing them with the ability to perceive their surroundings, navigate complex environments, and perform tasks with precision. This is achieved through the integration of sensors, such as cameras and LiDAR, with spatial algorithms that enable real-time decision-making.

Machine learning and AI
Machine learning and AI are fundamental to Spatial AI, providing the computational power and algorithms needed to process vast amounts of spatial data. Deep learning models, reinforcement learning, and neural networks are employed to train systems for tasks such as object recognition, spatial reasoning, and autonomous navigation. These models learn from large datasets, improving their accuracy and efficiency over time.

Spatial data processing
Spatial data processing involves the collection, analysis, and interpretation of data related to the physical world. This includes geospatial data, 3D models, and sensor data. Techniques such as SLAM, point cloud processing, and spatial indexing are used to map environments, track objects, and understand spatial relationships. Efficient spatial data processing is critical for real-time applications of Spatial AI.

3 Applications of Spatial AI

Autonomous vehicles
One of the most prominent applications of Spatial AI is in autonomous vehicles. Self-driving cars rely on spatial understanding to navigate roads, recognize traffic signs, and avoid obstacles. Spatial AI enables these vehicles to create detailed maps of their surroundings, interpret sensor data, and make split-second decisions to ensure safe and efficient transportation.

Augmented reality (AR) and virtual reality (VR)
Spatial AI plays a significant role in AR and VR, enhancing the user experience by creating immersive and interactive environments. In AR, spatial understanding allows for the seamless integration of digital objects with the real world, enabling applications in gaming, education, and industrial

training. In VR, Spatial AI enables realistic simulations of physical spaces, providing users with a sense of presence and immersion.

Smart cities

Smart cities leverage Spatial AI to improve urban infrastructure and services. Applications include traffic management, public safety, and environmental monitoring. By analyzing spatial data from sensors and cameras, Spatial AI can optimize traffic flow, detect anomalies, and manage resources efficiently. This contributes to the creation of sustainable and resilient urban environments.

Healthcare

In healthcare, Spatial AI is used for medical imaging, surgical assistance, and patient monitoring. Advanced computer vision algorithms help in the diagnosis of diseases by analyzing medical images such as X-rays, MRIs, and CT scans. Robots equipped with spatial understanding assist surgeons in

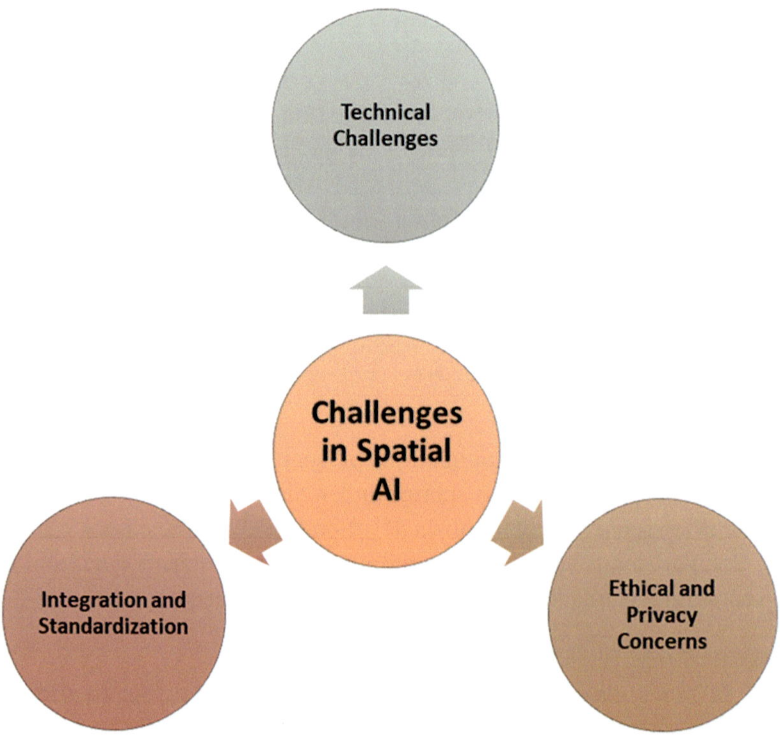

Figure 26.2 Challenges in spatial AI.

performing precise and minimally invasive procedures. Additionally, Spatial AI enables remote monitoring of patients, enhancing the quality of care.

Industrial automation
Spatial AI is revolutionizing industrial automation by enabling robots to perform complex tasks in dynamic environments. In manufacturing, robots equipped with spatial perception can assemble products, inspect quality, and manage inventory with high precision. Spatial AI also plays a role in logistics, where autonomous robots navigate warehouses, transport goods, and optimize supply chain operations.

4 Challenges in Spatial AI

Technical challenges
The development and deployment of Spatial AI face several technical challenges. These include the need for high computational power, real-time processing capabilities, and robust algorithms that can handle complex and dynamic environments. Ensuring the accuracy and reliability of spatial data is also a critical challenge, as errors in perception or mapping can lead to significant consequences.

Ethical and privacy concerns
The widespread use of Spatial AI raises ethical and privacy concerns. The collection and processing of spatial data, particularly in public spaces, can infringe on individuals' privacy. There is also the risk of misuse of spatial data for surveillance or other malicious purposes. Addressing these concerns requires the development of ethical guidelines and regulations to ensure the responsible use of Spatial AI.

Integration and standardization
Integrating Spatial AI systems with existing infrastructure and technologies poses significant challenges. The lack of standardization in spatial data formats, communication protocols, and interoperability can hinder the seamless integration of Spatial AI applications. Developing common standards and frameworks is essential to facilitate the widespread adoption of Spatial AI.

5 Future Prospects of Spatial AI

Advancements in technology
The future of Spatial AI is promising, with advancements in technology expected to drive its growth. Improvements in sensor technology,

computational power, and AI algorithms will enhance the capabilities of Spatial AI systems. Emerging technologies such as quantum computing and neuromorphic computing hold the potential to revolutionize spatial data processing and decision-making.

Potential impact on various industries

Spatial AI is poised to have a transformative impact on various industries. In transportation, the widespread adoption of autonomous vehicles will revolutionize mobility and logistics. In healthcare, Spatial AI will enable more accurate diagnostics, personalized treatments, and improved patient outcomes. The construction and real estate industries will benefit from enhanced planning, design, and maintenance of buildings and infrastructure.

Societal implications

The societal implications of Spatial AI are profound, with the potential to improve quality of life, increase efficiency, and drive economic growth. However, it also raises important questions about job displacement, equity, and access to technology. Ensuring that the benefits of Spatial AI are distributed fairly and addressing the societal challenges it presents will be crucial for its sustainable development.

What is next?

Spatial AI represents a significant leap forward in the integration of artificial intelligence with the physical world. By enabling machines to perceive, understand, and interact with their environment, Spatial AI opens up new possibilities across a wide range of applications. From autonomous vehicles to smart cities, Spatial AI is poised to transform industries and improve our daily lives. However, addressing the technical, ethical, and societal challenges will be essential to fully realizing the potential of Spatial AI. As technology continues to advance, the future of Spatial AI holds immense promise, paving the way for a smarter and more connected world.

27

Small Language Models (SLMs): Compact AI with Practical Applications

In the rapidly evolving field of natural language processing (NLP) and artificial intelligence (AI), large language models (LLMs) like GPT, PaLM, and Claude have captured the public's imagination with their impressive capabilities. These massive models, comprising billions or even trillions of parameters, can generate human-like text, answer complex queries, and even engage in creative tasks like writing stories or poetry.

However, alongside these behemoth models, a different class of AI systems has been quietly gaining traction: small language models (SLM). As their name implies, these models are significantly smaller in size, often with

DOI: 10.1201/9788743812999-27

fewer than a billion parameters. While they may not match the sheer power of their larger counterparts, small language models offer a unique set of advantages that make them well-suited for various practical applications.

1 What are Small Language Models?

Small language models are a type of *neural network designed to process and generate human language*. Like their larger counterparts, they are trained on vast amounts of text data, allowing them to learn patterns, relationships, and nuances within language. However, their smaller size means they require fewer *computational resources*, making them more efficient and easier to deploy in various environments, including *edge devices* and *mobile applications*.

One of the key advantages of small language models is their *efficiency*. Because they have fewer parameters, they require less memory and processing power, which translates to faster inference times and lower energy consumption. This efficiency makes them particularly attractive for applications where real-time performance or resource constraints are critical, such as virtual assistants, chatbots, and embedded systems.

Another benefit of small language models is their potential for better *interpretability* and *transparency*. While LLMs are often criticized for being "black boxes" due to their complexity, smaller models may be more amenable to analysis and explanation, allowing researchers and developers to better understand their decision-making processes.

2 Applications of Small Language Models

Small language models have found applications in a wide range of domains, leveraging their efficiency and specialized capabilities. Here are some notable examples as shown in Figure 27.1.

1. **Virtual assistants and chatbots:** One of the most prominent applications of small language models is in the development of virtual assistants and chatbots. These conversational AI systems need to respond in real-time to user inputs, making efficiency a critical factor. Small language models can provide quick and relevant responses while operating within the resource constraints of mobile devices or embedded systems.
2. **Text summarization:** Summarizing long documents or articles in a concise and coherent manner is a challenging task for AI systems. Small language models have shown promising results in this area, distilling

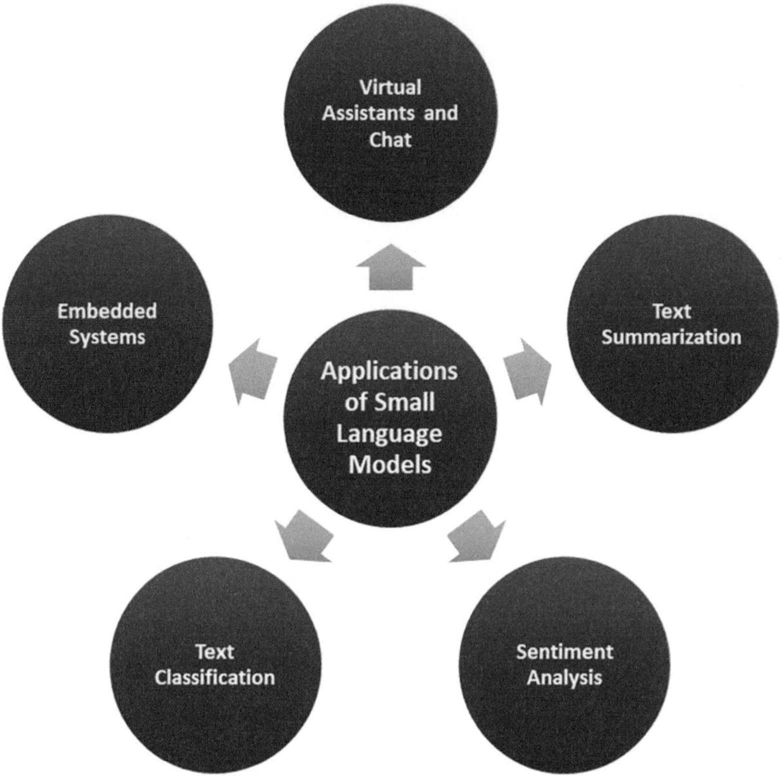

Figure 27.1 Applications of small language models.

key information from lengthy texts into concise summaries. Their compact size makes them well-suited for deployment in applications such as news aggregators, research tools, and content curation platforms.

3. **Sentiment analysis:** Understanding the sentiment expressed in text is crucial for various applications, including social media monitoring, customer feedback analysis, and brand reputation management. Small language models can be trained to accurately classify text as positive, negative, or neutral, providing valuable insights into public opinion and consumer sentiment.

4. **Text classification:** Beyond sentiment analysis, small language models can be employed for broader text classification tasks, such as categorizing documents by topic, identifying spam or offensive content, or triaging customer support inquiries. Their efficiency and specialized

training make them valuable tools for automating and streamlining various text-based workflows.

5. **Embedded systems:** and Internet of Things (IoT) With the rise of the Internet of Things (IoT), there is an increasing demand for AI capabilities in resource-constrained devices and edge computing environments. Small language models can be embedded in these systems, enabling intelligent language processing and generation for applications like voice assistants, smart home devices, and industrial automation.

3 Comparing Small Language Models to LLMs

While small language models offer several advantages, it is important to compare them to their larger counterparts (LLMs) to understand their relative strengths and limitations.

1. **Performance and capabilities:** LLMs, with their vast parameter counts and extensive training data, generally outperform small language models in terms of raw performance on various NLP tasks. They can handle more complex and open-ended queries, exhibit better language understanding and generation capabilities, and excel at tasks like question answering, text summarization, and creative writing.

   However, small language models can sometimes match or even surpass the performance of LLMs on specific, narrowly defined tasks for which they have been optimized. Their compact size allows for efficient fine-tuning and specialization, making them well-suited for targeted applications.

2. **Resource requirements:** One of the most significant advantages of small language models is their efficiency in terms of computational resources. They require significantly less memory, processing power, and energy than LLMs, making them more practical for deployment in resource-constrained environments, such as mobile devices, embedded systems, and edge computing platforms.

   LLMs, on the other hand, often require substantial hardware resources, including powerful GPUs or specialized accelerators. This can make them more expensive to deploy and maintain, particularly in scenarios where real-time performance or on-device processing is required.

3. **Interpretability and transparency:** While LLMs are often criticized for their opacity and lack of interpretability, small language models may offer improved transparency and explainability. Their simpler architectures and fewer parameters can make it easier to analyze and

understand their decision-making processes, potentially leading to more trustworthy and accountable AI systems.

However, it is important to note that even small language models can exhibit complex behavior and biases, and efforts to improve interpretability remain an active area of research.

4. **Training and customization:** LLMs require vast amounts of training data and computational resources to achieve their impressive performance. This can make them challenging and expensive to train from scratch or fine-tune for specific tasks or domains.

   Small language models, on the other hand, can often be trained or fine-tuned more efficiently, using smaller datasets and fewer computational resources. This flexibility makes them more accessible for customization and adaptation to specific use cases or domains, particularly for organizations with limited resources.

5. **Privacy and security:** The massive size of LLMs can raise privacy and security concerns, as they may inadvertently memorize and potentially reveal sensitive information from their training data. Small language models, with their more limited capacity, may be less prone to such issues, making them more suitable for applications involving sensitive or confidential data.

   However, it is important to note that privacy and security considerations apply to all AI systems, and appropriate measures must be taken to protect user data and ensure responsible deployment.

4 The Future of Small Language Models

As AI technology continues to advance, the role and potential of small language models are likely to evolve. Here are some potential future developments as shown in Figure 27.2.

1. **Specialized models:** While LLMs aim for broad capabilities, small language models may become increasingly specialized and optimized for specific tasks or domains. We may see the emergence of highly efficient models tailored for applications like medical diagnosis, legal document analysis, or financial forecasting.

2. **Composable AI:** Small language models could become building blocks in larger, modular AI systems, where different components handle specialized tasks and work together to achieve complex goals. This

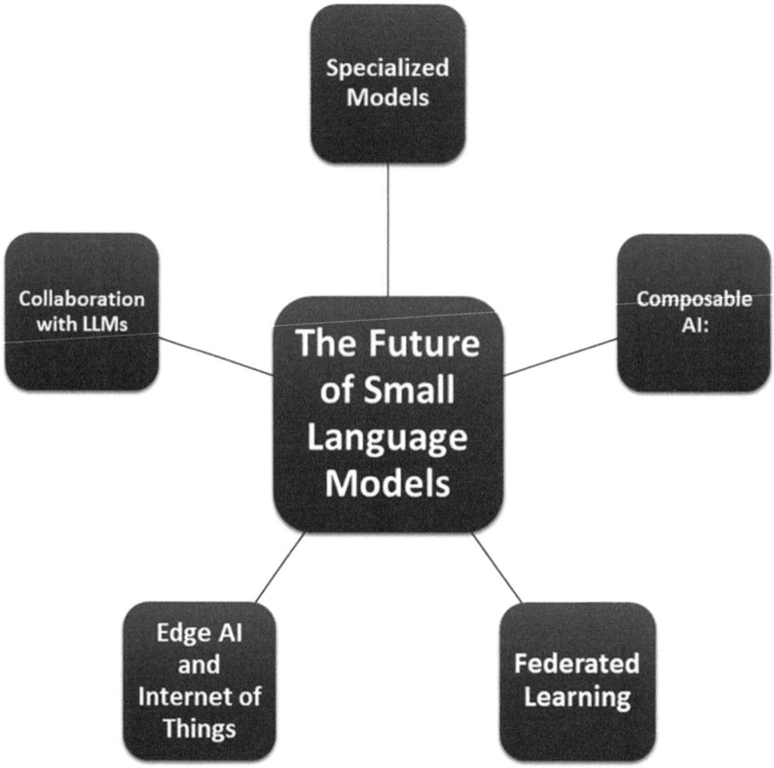

Figure 27.2 The future of small language models.

"composable AI" approach could leverage the strengths of small models while mitigating their limitations.

3. **Federated learning:** Privacy and data ownership concerns may drive the development of federated learning techniques, where small language models are trained on decentralized data sources without the need for centralized data collection. This could enable more privacy-preserving and secure AI deployments.

4. **Edge AI and Internet of Things:** As the Internet of Things continues to expand, the demand for intelligent language processing capabilities in edge devices and resource-constrained environments will grow. Small language models are well-positioned to power these applications, enabling real-time language processing and generation on the edge.

5. **Collaboration with LLMs:** While small language models and LLMs may seem like competing approaches, they could potentially complement each other in hybrid systems. For example, a small model could handle initial processing and filtering, offloading more complex tasks to a larger model when necessary, optimizing resource usage and performance.

In the rapidly evolving landscape of natural language processing and AI, small language models offer a compelling alternative to their larger counterparts. While they may not match the sheer power and capabilities of LLMs, their efficiency, interpretability, and specialized performance make them valuable tools for a wide range of practical applications.

As AI technology continues to advance, small language models are likely to play an increasingly important role, powering intelligent language processing and generation in resource-constrained environments, enabling edge AI and Internet of Things applications, and potentially serving as building blocks in larger, modular AI systems.

Moreover, the development of specialized small language models, federated learning techniques, and hybrid approaches combining small and large models could further unlock their potential and address emerging challenges in areas like privacy, security, and efficiency.

Ultimately, the future of AI is likely to be one of diversity, where different types of models, including small language models and LLMs, coexist and collaborate to tackle the complex challenges of natural language processing and beyond.

28

Large Behavior Models (LBMs): The Next Frontier in Artificial Intelligence

Artificial intelligence (AI) has rapidly transformed from a niche academic field to a driving force of the global economy, society, and culture. Central to this revolution are large language models (LLMs) like OpenAI's GPT series, Google's Gemini, and Anthropic's Claude. These models have demonstrated a remarkable capacity to understand and generate human language, allowing machines to write essays, code software, compose music, and hold convincing conversations.

Yet, while LLMs excel in manipulating text, they do not inherently understand behavior. They can describe what someone might do, but they

DOI: 10.1201/9788743812999-28

do not model actual human actions, sequences, decisions, or context-based responses. This gap between *language* and *action* – between what is said and what is done – is where a new class of AI models emerges: *Large behavior models (LBMs)*.

LBMs are poised to revolutionize AI by moving beyond text into the realm of *decision-making, behavioral prediction, interaction, and simulation*. These models will not only predict what you might say, but what you might do, how you will respond in various environments, and how agents (human or artificial) interact with one another in dynamic, realistic, and goal-driven ways.

This article explores the definition, architecture, applications, challenges, and future implications of LBMs, positioning them as the logical next step in the evolution of intelligent systems.

1 What is a Large Behavior Model?

A *large behavior model (LBM)* is an AI system trained on vast amounts of behavioral data – spanning physical actions, decisions, emotional reactions, social interactions, and contextual responses – designed to understand, predict, and simulate complex agent behavior in dynamic environments.

While LLMs operate primarily on textual data (what people say), LBMs operate on *multimodal behavioral data* (what people do, how they act, how they respond over time). They can be trained using video, sensor data, logs of physical movement, time series of actions, environmental inputs, decision trees, and even neurophysiological signals.

LBMs aim to develop *embodied intelligence* – AI that interacts with the world not just through a keyboard or screen, but through physical, social, and temporal engagement. They are a cornerstone in the development of *artificial general intelligence (AGI)*, because general intelligence requires general behavior: the ability to learn, adapt, act, and interact across situations.

2 Why Behavior Matters in AI

Humans are not merely linguistic creatures. We are behavioral beings – moving through space, forming habits, solving problems, collaborating in teams, navigating challenges, and adapting to change. Understanding human behavior is key to building machines that can coexist with us.

Language models can simulate empathy in writing, but cannot exhibit *true empathetic behavior* without modeling physical and emotional context. They can describe how to play a game, but cannot *play* it unless they can model the sequence of actions, rewards, and consequences. A chatbot might give you advice about fitness, but without behavioral modeling, it cannot adapt to your habits, routines, and environment.

Behavior is where *intention, memory, perception, and action* converge. LBMs integrate these dimensions to simulate a fuller spectrum of intelligence.

3 Building Blocks of Large Behavior Models

Creating an LBM requires integrating several technologies and methodologies, each contributing to its ability to observe, simulate, and generate behavior.

Multimodal data ingestion
LBMs rely on data far beyond text. They must ingest and process:

- Video of people interacting in various contexts (e.g., classrooms, offices, hospitals)
- Motion capture and sensor data from wearables
- Logs from software systems showing sequences of actions
- Decision outcomes from games, simulations, or real-world processes
- Environmental cues such as objects, lighting, temperature, or social proximity

This diversity of input enables LBMs to build rich, contextual representations of environments and agent states.

Behavioral embedding spaces
Just as LLMs learn word embeddings that represent meaning, LBMs must develop *behavioral embeddings* – mathematical representations of actions, decisions, routines, and preferences. These embeddings allow the model to compare, predict, and cluster behaviors across individuals and scenarios.

For instance, "greeting a coworker" might be represented differently depending on culture, context, time of day, and prior history – but all would map to similar points in a behavioral embedding space.

Temporal memory and context
Behavior unfolds over time. LBMs must maintain a *temporal memory* of past actions and anticipated future outcomes. This allows them to generate consistent and coherent behavior across time spans – from seconds

(e.g., conversation flow) to weeks (e.g., project planning) to years (e.g., lifestyle modeling).

Goal-directed decision frameworks
Many LBMs incorporate *reinforcement learning*, which trains agents to take actions that maximize cumulative rewards in simulated environments. This decision-making capacity is crucial for models that must not only describe but also *choose* behaviors.

4 Applications of LBMs

The potential applications of LBMs span nearly every domain where human behavior matters.

Digital humans and virtual assistants
LBMs can power digital characters that remember your preferences, adapt their routines to your needs, and behave with lifelike consistency. These digital humans could become companions, coaches, tutors, or even therapists, behaving not just with verbal competence but also with emotional intelligence and behavioral continuity.

Simulation and planning
Government, military, and industrial actors can use LBMs to simulate human or group behavior in scenarios such as:

- Evacuation planning in natural disasters
- Crowd control in public spaces
- Battlefield simulations
- Urban development planning
- Market reaction simulations

By modeling how thousands of agents behave in parallel, LBMs provide powerful foresight into complex systems.

Robotics and embodied AI
For robots to interact effectively in homes, hospitals, or workplaces, they must understand and predict human behavior. LBMs allow robots to navigate social norms, anticipate human actions, and adjust their own behavior

accordingly. A robot nurse, for instance, could approach a patient based on behavioral cues of discomfort or stress.

Education and personalized learning
AI tutors powered by LBMs could observe student behaviors over time – engagement levels, attention spans, hesitation patterns – and adapt instruction methods to optimize learning. They could simulate classroom environments for teacher training or even role-play student personas to help educators prepare.

Behavior-based cybersecurity
In digital systems, human behavior leaves traces – login patterns, mouse movements, workflow sequences. LBMs can learn normal behavioral patterns and detect anomalies that suggest insider threats, fraud, or cyberattacks. This shift from rule-based to behavior-based security is already underway in sectors like finance and defense.

Consumer behavior and market research
By modeling consumer decision-making behavior – not just from surveys, but from real-time interactions – companies can better understand customer journeys, loyalty drivers, and purchase intentions. LBMs could simulate how a new product might perform under different economic or cultural conditions.

5 The Science Behind LBMs

LBMs are not built from scratch; they evolve from decades of AI research, as shown in Figure 28.1:

- **Cognitive architectures:** Frameworks like ACT-R, Soar, and Leabra attempted to model human cognition and behavior. LBMs build on these ideas with neural network power.
- **Reinforcement learning agents:** From DeepMind's AlphaGo to OpenAI's Dota agents, behavior modeling in games laid the groundwork for real-world simulations.
- **Transformer architectures:** The success of LLMs using transformers has led to multimodal transformers like Gato, Flamingo, and Gemini, which serve as architectural blueprints for LBMs.

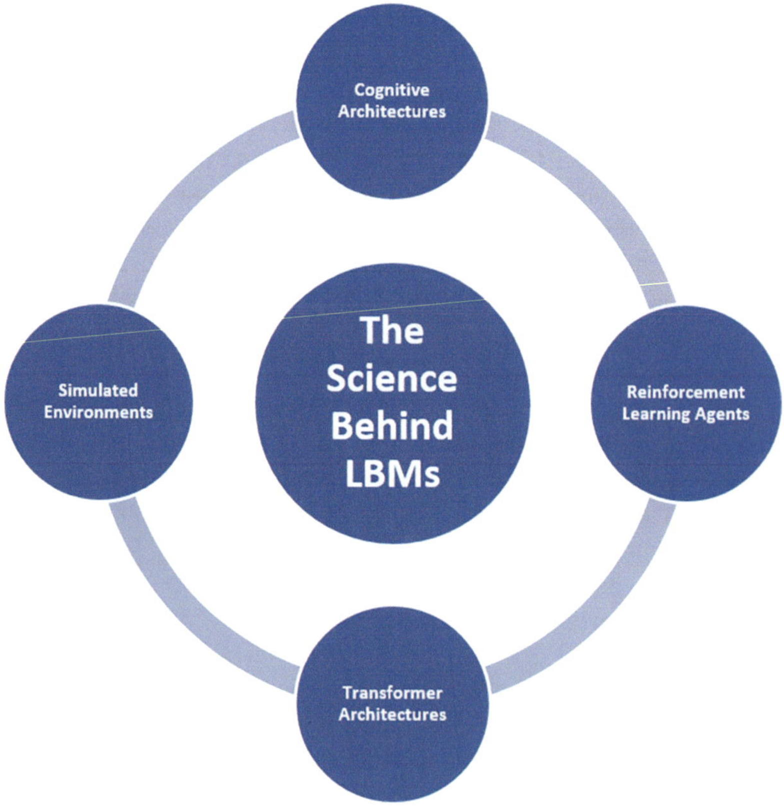

Figure 28.1 The science behind LBMs.

- **Simulated environments:** Tools like Minecraft, MuJoCo, Habitat, and CARLA allow AI agents to practice behaviors in sandbox worlds before applying them in real ones.

6 Ethical and Social Implications

As with any transformative technology, LBMs raise profound questions about privacy, control, bias, and responsibility.

Behavioral surveillance

If LBMs are trained on data from surveillance cameras, smart devices, or social platforms, who owns that behavioral data? Could it be used to manipulate, profile, or punish individuals? The line between personalization and coercion becomes dangerously thin.

Bias in behavior modeling
Training data reflects the biases of the societies from which it is drawn. If LBMs learn from discriminatory or exclusionary behavior, they may reproduce or amplify those patterns – whether in hiring simulations, policing models, or digital companions.

Autonomy and free will
If an AI can predict your behavior better than you can, does that compromise your autonomy? Could LBMs be used to influence choices in subtle ways – from advertising to political persuasion?

Simulated humans
As LBMs create increasingly realistic digital humans, how do we distinguish between real and artificial behavior? Could this blur the boundaries of identity, consent, and trust?

7 Toward Artificial General Behavior

Many experts believe that the road to artificial general intelligence (AGI) will run through *artificial general behavior (AGB)* – the capacity of an AI to act sensibly across domains, goals, and environments.

LLMs are one component of this; LBMs are another. Together, they enable AI systems to perceive reason, communicate, and act in human-like ways. The next generation of AI will not just be intelligent – it will be *agentic*: goal-directed, behaviorally autonomous, and contextually aware.

8 The Future of LBMs: Predictions

Over the next decade, LBMs are likely to evolve along the following lines:

- **More real-time adaptability:** LBMs will be able to adapt to new environments on the fly, using a combination of pretraining and continual learning.
- **Emotionally aware behavior:** Models will detect and respond to emotional states, enabling more compassionate and human-centered AI.

- **Cross-agent modeling:** LBMs will simulate multiple agents interacting in shared environments, leading to advances in group behavior, cooperation, and social simulation.
- **Behavioral APIs:** Developers will use LBMs via APIs to add "behavioral realism" to applications, just as they use LLMs today for text.
- **Regulation and policy:** Governments will begin to regulate how behavioral data can be collected, modeled, and used – especially in surveillance and predictive policing contexts.

Behavior is the missing link

The story of AI has long focused on perception (computer vision, speech recognition) and language (LLMs). But human intelligence is not just about seeing and saying – it is about *doing*.

Large behavior models represent the next phase in AI's evolution: an effort to build systems that do not merely speak or observe but act, adapt, learn from consequences, and interact over time.

By bridging the gap between *knowing* and *doing*, LBMs bring us closer to AI that can truly share our world – not just as tools, but as intelligent partners in action.

Whether assisting doctors in surgery, guiding students in classrooms, managing cities, or exploring other planets, LBMs will define a future where behavior itself becomes programmable, predictable, and – if we are wise – ethical and human-centered.

29

Why Companies Fail in Their AI Projects: Lessons from the Frontlines

Artificial intelligence (AI) has been hailed as the transformative force of the 21st century, promising to revolutionize industries from healthcare to finance, retail to manufacturing. Organizations worldwide have rushed to integrate AI into their strategies, with global spending on AI systems expected to surpass $300 billion by 2030. Yet despite the excitement and enormous investment, studies reveal a sobering reality: *up to 95% of AI projects fail to deliver on their intended objectives, according to a recent study by MIT.*

Why do so many AI projects fall short? Is it the complexity of the technology, the lack of talent, or unrealistic expectations? We will explore the

DOI: 10.1201/9788743812999-29

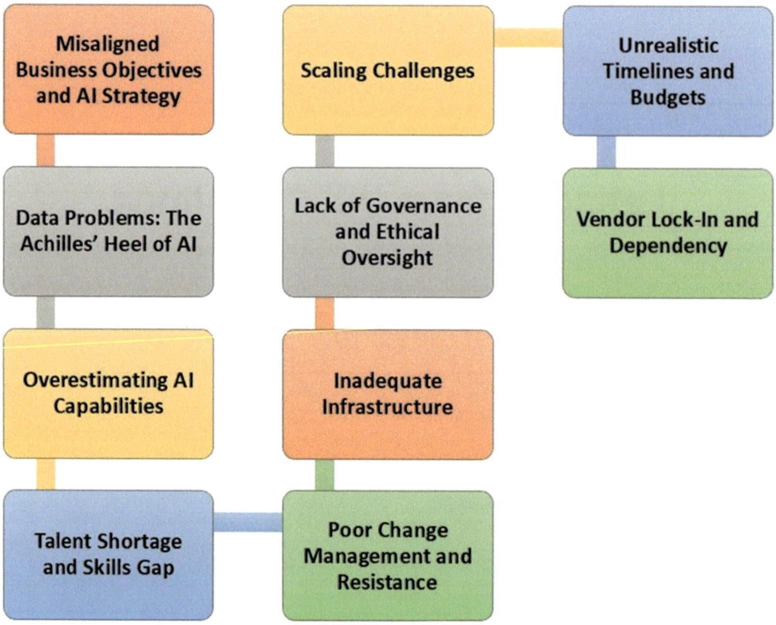

Figure 29.1 Why AI projects fail?

core reasons behind AI project failures, offering a structured analysis supported by industry examples and actionable insights.

1 Misaligned Business Objectives and AI Strategy

The first and perhaps most fundamental reason for failure is the *disconnect between AI initiatives and business goals*. Many companies embark on AI projects because it is trendy or because competitors are doing it, not because they have identified a specific business problem AI can solve.

Common issues

- **Lack of clarity:** AI is often treated as a goal rather than a tool to achieve measurable outcomes.
- **No ROI mapping:** Organizations fail to define how AI will impact key performance indicators (KPIs).

Example
A retail chain invests in AI-powered chatbots to improve customer service but does not integrate the bot with inventory systems. As a result, the bot

cannot answer questions about product availability, frustrating customers and increasing support costs.

Lesson: Align AI with core business objectives from the start. Define success metrics tied to revenue, cost reduction, or customer experience.

2 Data Problems: The Achilles' Heel of AI

AI thrives on data. Without high-quality, relevant, and sufficient data, even the most sophisticated models will underperform.

Common data challenges

- **Poor data quality:** Missing values, duplicates, and inaccuracies undermine model accuracy.
- **Data silos:** Different departments hoard data, creating fragmented datasets.
- **Lack of diversity:** Biased or incomplete datasets lead to biased predictions.
- **Data governance:** No clear policies on ownership, security, or compliance (e.g., GDPR).

Example
A financial institution attempted to deploy a credit risk model trained on historical data that did not account for gig economy workers. The result? High rejection rates for qualified applicants lead to customer backlash and regulatory scrutiny.

Lesson: Invest in data cleaning, governance, and infrastructure before building AI models.

3 Overestimating AI Capabilities

The hype surrounding AI leads many executives to believe that the technology is a silver bullet. *Overpromising and underdelivering* are recurring themes in failed AI projects.

Common pitfalls

- Expecting AI to provide 100% accuracy.
- Believing AI can replace human judgment in complex, ambiguous situations.

- Misunderstanding AI's limitations in reasoning, context awareness, and adaptability.

Example
A healthcare startup promised an AI diagnostic tool capable of outperforming doctors. However, the tool failed in real-world scenarios due to variability in patient data and clinical workflows.

Lesson: Set realistic expectations and educate stakeholders on what AI can and cannot do.

4 Talent Shortage and Skills Gap

AI is complex, requiring expertise in *machine learning, data engineering, cloud computing, and domain knowledge*. The shortage of AI talent is acute, and even when talent is available, it may not be integrated effectively into the organization.

Issues

- **Overreliance on external vendors:** Companies outsource everything, losing control over IP and strategy.
- **Lack of interdisciplinary teams:** Data scientists work in isolation without input from business or IT teams.
- **Insufficient training:** Employees do not understand how to use or trust AI systems.

Example
A global bank hired top AI engineers but did not train its business analysts to interpret AI outputs, resulting in underutilized models and wasted investment.

Lesson: Build cross-functional teams and invest in upskilling employees.

5 Poor Change Management and Resistance

AI adoption disrupts workflows, roles, and organizational culture. Resistance from employees – often driven by fear of job loss – can derail even the most promising AI initiatives.

Key barriers

- **Fear and mistrust:** Employees worry about automation replacing jobs.
- **Lack of transparency:** Black-box models fuel skepticism.

- **Weak leadership:** Leaders fail to champion AI adoption and communicate its benefits.

Example
A manufacturing firm introduced AI-driven predictive maintenance, but technicians resisted using the system, fearing it would eliminate their roles. As a result, the system was ignored, and machine downtime persisted.

Lesson: Involve stakeholders early, explain the value, and provide reassurance through training and communication.

6 Inadequate Infrastructure

AI models require powerful computing resources, scalable storage, and seamless integration with existing systems. Many organizations underestimate the infrastructure requirements.

Issues

- **Legacy systems:** Old IT architecture cannot handle AI workloads.
- **Insufficient cloud adoption:** On-premises systems lack flexibility for AI scaling.
- **Integration challenges:** AI tools fail to connect with ERP, CRM, and other business platforms.

Example
An e-commerce company deployed an AI recommendation engine, but due to poor integration with its order management system, recommendations were delayed, resulting in a negative user experience.

Lesson: Upgrade infrastructure and plan for integration from day one.

7 Lack of Governance and Ethical Oversight

AI introduces ethical, legal, and compliance challenges. Companies that ignore these concerns face reputational damage and regulatory penalties.

Risks

- **Bias and discrimination:** AI decisions that disadvantage certain groups.
- **Privacy violations:** Improper handling of sensitive data.
- **Regulatory noncompliance:** Violations of GDPR, CCPA, or sector-specific rules.

Example
A recruitment platform faced a lawsuit after its AI system was found to favor male candidates over female candidates due to biased historical data.

Lesson: Establish an AI ethics framework and comply with regulations.

8 Scaling Challenges

Building a proof of concept is easy; scaling AI across an enterprise is not. Many projects fail during the transition from prototype to production.

Challenges

- **Operationalization:** Lack of MLOps pipelines for continuous deployment and monitoring.
- **Cost overruns:** Scaling requires massive investment in compute and storage.
- **Inconsistent adoption:** Different departments adopt AI unevenly, creating inefficiencies.

Example
A telecom company successfully piloted an AI-driven churn prediction model in one region but failed to roll it out nationwide due to incompatible systems and a lack of coordination.

Lesson: Plan for scalability and adopt MLOps best practices.

9 Unrealistic Timelines and Budgets

AI projects often take longer and cost more than anticipated. Failure to account for iteration cycles, data preparation, and regulatory checks leads to frustration and project abandonment.

Example
A logistics firm budgeted six months for an AI route optimization project. It took 18 months due to unexpected data integration issues, and the project was eventually scrapped.

Lesson: Build realistic timelines and include buffer periods for experimentation.

10 Vendor Lock-In and Dependency

Organizations often become overly dependent on specific vendors or platforms, limiting flexibility and innovation.

Risks

- **Cost escalation:** Vendors raise prices after initial adoption.
- **Limited control:** Companies cannot customize solutions.
- **Exit barriers:** Migrating to another platform is expensive and complex.

Lesson: Opt for open standards and multi-cloud strategies.

11 Turning Failure into Success

AI is not a magic wand; it is a tool that requires *strategic alignment, quality data, talent, infrastructure, and cultural readiness*. Companies that succeed in AI adoption share common traits:

- Clear business objectives tied to measurable ROI.
- Robust data governance and infrastructure.
- Cross-functional teams and strong leadership.
- Transparent communication and ethical practices.

The road to AI success is challenging, but failure is not inevitable. By learning from these common mistakes and adopting a structured, realistic approach, organizations can unlock the full potential of AI and gain a competitive edge in the digital economy.

Index

About the Author

Prof. Ahmed Banafa is a globally recognized expert in the fields of *artificial intelligence (AI), Blockchain, Cybersecurity, and the Internet of Things (IoT).* With a distinguished career that spans research, operations, and strategic technology management, he has been a prominent voice in shaping the discourse around emerging technologies.

He has received numerous accolades for his work, including the *Certificate of Honor from the City and County of San Francisco*, the *Haskell Award for Distinguished Teaching from the University of Massachusetts Lowell*, and the prestigious *Author & Artist Award from San Jose State University*. In 2018, *LinkedIn named him the No. 1 Tech Voice to Follow*, highlighting his foresight and influence in technology trends.

Prof. Banafa's thought leadership has been featured in *Time, Nature, Forbes, IEEE Spectrum*, and the *MIT Technology Review*. He has been a guest expert on global media outlets such as *ABC, CBS, NBC, FOX, Bloomberg, BBC, NPR, Reuters, and NHK*, providing insights on cutting-edge technology topics. He is also a contributing member of the *MIT Technology Review Global Panel*, further cementing his role as a respected thought leader.

An accomplished author, Prof. Banafa has written several acclaimed books, including:

- *Secure and Smart Internet of Things (IoT) Using Blockchain and Artificial Intelligence (AI)* – Winner of the SJSU Author and Artist Award and ranked among the *Best Technology Books of All Time*.
- *Blockchain Technology and Applications* – Adopted into curricula at prestigious universities, including Stanford.
- *Quantum Computing* – Officially added to the *Library of Congress* collection.

- *Transformative AI* and *Introduction to AI* (2025) – Both received the SJSU Author and Artist Award.
- His upcoming work, *AI in Action*, marks his ninth book and explores AI's real-world impact across industries.

Prof. Banafa studied *Cybersecurity at Harvard University* and *Digital Transformation at the Massachusetts Institute of Technology (MIT)*. He holds a *master's degree in Electrical Engineering* and a *Ph.D. in Artificial Intelligence*.

For Product Safety Concerns and Information please contact our
EU representative GPSR@taylorandfrancis.com Taylor & Francis
Verlag GmbH, Kaufingerstraße 24, 80331 München, Germany